Debrett's Book of Antiques

'The Resurrection' by Dieric Bouts. On April 16th 1980 it fetched £1,700,000, the highest price for which Sotheby's had, up until that time, ever sold any item at auction.

DEBRETT'S Book of ANTIQUES

Edited and compiled by

Patrick Macnaghten

Preface by

Bevis Hillier

Debrett's Peerage Limited

Published by Debrett's Peerage Ltd.,
73/77 Britannia Road, London SW6

ISBN 0 905649 33 8

Designed by SINC
Printed in Great Britain by Waterlow
(Dunstable) Ltd.

Contents

We are grateful to the following for supplying illustrations.

Thomas Agnew and Sons Limited
43 Old Bond Street
London W1

Barling of Mount Street Limited
112 Mount Street
London W1Y 5HE

W and F C Bonham and Sons Limited
Montpelier Galleries
Montpelier Street
London SW7 1HH

Christie Manson and Woods Limited
8 King Street
London SW1

Michael G Cox
Market Place
Tetbury
Gloucestershire GL8 8DF

Robson Lowe Limited
50 Pall Mall
London SW1 5JZ

Madeleine Pearson
c/o The Contemporary Arts Society
Tate Gallery
London SW1

Phillips
Blenstock House
7 Blenheim Street
New Bond Street
London W1 0AS

Barrie Quinn Jardinieres Limited
1, 3 and 4 Broxholme House
New Kings Road
London SW6

B A Seaby Limited
Audley House
11 Margaret Street
London W1N 8AT

Sotheby Parke Bernet and Co
34 New Bond Street
London W1

Foreword
by Bevis Hillier

THE use of the French word 'amateur' to mean 'collector', which was common in England during the eighteenth century, has almost entirely gone out. This indicates something more than a mere fashion in vocabulary. Collecting itself has changed, and the *amateur* has been succeeded by the professional. We are no longer content to make pleasant speculations about the factory of a piece of porcelain: we go and excavate the factory site, and see whether the old fragments and 'shards' that we dig up match the whole (or nearly whole) pieces of china on our shelves.

It is right that this should happen. Discovering the truth about an antique is more satisfying than the fanciest of guesses. Too often the devotees of 'blue china' in the late nineteenth century bought export ginger-jars and thought they had acquired the treasures of the ancients. In 1957 the late Arthur Lane, Keeper of the Department of Ceramics at the Victoria and Albert Museum, made fun of the vagueness of his predecessors, in a paper read to the English Ceramic Circle:

> Those were the days of wild, romantic speculation. I note one entry [in the Museum records]: 'Vase with grey crackled glaze. Ancient Chinese.' (I have pursued this piece, and find that we have now prosaically labelled it 'Chinese; about 1800-1820'.)

At the same time, we have lost something by the decline of the amateur in antique-collecting. Today a collection is too often a range of 'specimens', to be 'inspected' like an entomologist's beetles. At least the old romantic kind of collector, with all his laziness about factories and dates and his rather maudlin gloating over glazes and marks, had some sense of the aesthetic appeal of his collection, or of its value as physical relics of the past, 'talismans' of history. The difference between the two kinds of collecting might be compared to two owners of golden retrievers. One investigates the pedigree, has the heart tested, makes sure the forehead is of the right breadth. The other treats the dog as a pet and becomes very fond of it. Of course, there is no reason why one should not do *both* things: and that is where I think this book, edited by Patrick Macnaghten, succeeds so well. He has brought together distinguished experts and shameless amateurs (he himself cheerfully admits to being an amateur—though I suspect that in many years of inquiring amateur collecting, he has virtually turned himself into an expert, and on many subjects.)

Certainly the experts predominate in this book. The thing about an expert is that he can boil his subject down to its essentials:

nobody else knows what it is right to discard. At the risk of making odious comparisons, I would single out Anthony Hobson's chapter on book collecting as a model of its kind, a piece of prose as beautifully turned as anything by his friend, the late Cyril Connolly—and brimming with germane facts as well as with delightful and provocative ideas. Robert Darley-Doran is another expert who writes with relaxed familiarity about his subject, bringing home to us the elements of coin collecting with evocative phrases such as 'the unselfconscious beauty' of ancient Greek coinage, or showing us how coinage was 'a tool of political propaganda' for the emperors of ancient Rome. I enjoyed his pressing the candidacy of Croesus, king of Lydia, as the first coin collector. Ian Bennett ruthlessly divides that subject of bewildering complexity, oriental carpets and rugs, into easily assimilable rudiments—something I have not seen achieved by any other writer. And one of the most enjoyable of all the chapters is that by Michael Frostick on collectors' cars. At last I have gained some understanding of the difference between 'vintage', 'veteran' and 'classic' automobiles, and some of Michael Frostick's quips deserve to end up in the *Oxford Dictionary of Quotations*—for example: 'There is a certain steadfast agreement about how much the things are worth—the higher figures being those favoured by the owners, and the lower by the aspiring purchasers.' That, of course, applies to all antiques, not just to cars.

Cars (of which the majority of 'collectable' examples belong to the present century) are among the new subjects received, or about to be received, into the world of antiques. This extension of the frontiers of the 'antique', even more than the increased professionalism of collectors, is the biggest change which has overtaken collecting. The first book I ever bought on old pottery and porcelain, my first love, was George Savage's *Ceramics for the Collector* (1949). Near the end of this book, he wrote:

> I personally do not regard any English pottery after about 1770 as artistically valuable, but opinions differ . . . .By 1800, English pottery was rapidly approaching the doldrums, in which it wallowed uncomfortably throughout the nineteenth century. For that matter so did most of the arts in most countries, the art of the Impressionist painters in France providing one of the few bright spots.

Later in the book, he stated that 'collectors' pieces are all prior to 1800', and suggested that the nineteenth century 'may, in a few years time, seem little more than an unpleasant nightmare.' How hopelessly wrong he was! Since then, collectors have competed keenly for Victorian wares of the Great Exhibition period, for Art Nouveau, for the grotesqueries of Martinware, and lately, even for Doulton toby-jugs of the 1920s and 30s.

A similar change has taken place in the appreciation of silver. E. Alfred Jones wrote in his *Old Silver of Europe and America* (1928) that 'If the zeal for collecting persists, the conjecture may be made that some of the work of Paul Storr will in future ages be regarded by collectors with the same awe and admiration as that of Paul Lamerie today in England or Paul Revere in America.' Jones was right, even though he himself did not care for the massiveness and floridity of Regency silver. What he could not foresee was that in half a century's time, Great Exhibition silver would be avidly collected, also Elkington electro-plate, Art Nouveau wares by Archibald Knox, and even silver of the very time at which he was writing, by the great French master Puiforcat.

The same unrolling of frontiers has taken place in most collecting subjects. So, as Anne Crane points out in her chapter on glass, we have the extraordinary situation that the record price for a piece of glass is not for some iridescent Roman vial, nor for a vessel teased into fanciful shapes by a Venetian craftsman, nor a 'crizzled' goblet of the seventeenth century by our own Ravenscroft, but a nineteenth-century copy of the Portland Vase by John Northwood. Fashion as well as brute economics has something to do with the reception into the vexed category of 'collectors' pieces' of some previously despised antiques. The 'back to nature' movement of the late 1960s and early 70s, with its insistence on 'organic' foods, 'ethnic' clothes and 'recycling', may have helped to bring into popularity the attractive village rugs mentioned by Ian Bennett, or encouraged the move away from sophisticated French eighteenth-century weavings in favour of 'the simpler, more rustic charms of Flemish seventeenth-century "verdure" tapestries' noted by J. D. Mayorcas in his chapter on textiles. (And, incidentally, he remarks that a comparable symposium on antiques ten years ago would have contained no chapter on textiles and tapestries at all: another sign of changing attitudes.)

A new social awareness has entered collecting. We used to be interested only in who made what: which factory made the porcelain, which *hausmaler* decorated it; which *ébéniste* produced the furniture—and so on. Today many collectors are equally interested in the people for whom the ceramics and furniture were made. What sort of classes used pewter and who had silver on the table? This kind of approach to collecting, a perfectly valid one, tends to lessen the importance of aesthetics, the physical beauty of objects. Those who are concerned only with the 'quality' of things deplore this tendency: they include the 'brownwood men' who sell polished mahogany of the eighteenth century and little else. What these supercilious gentlemen forget is that many of us cannot afford Queen Anne card-tables or Georgian pedimented cabinets. That is why the Ephemera Society has been so popular: for a modest regular expenditure, it is possible to build up a collection which, while of no 'quality' in the brownwood sense, is attractive and tells us, cumulatively, something about the past. Even a collection of old luggage labels can do this.

The two great collecting subjects which have supervened in the last ten years—for which Sotheby's and Christie's have had to set up new salerooms and issue new categories of catalogues—are Art Nouveau and Art Deco. In both these subjects there are prizes and pickings for those who want quality *and* those who want social interest at not too great a cost. Nobody can deny the superb quality of the best Majorelle furniture, Gallé glass, Tiffany glass, Lalique jewellery, Ruhlmann furniture, Puiforcat silver, Templier jewellery or Kieffer book-bindings. But equally, John Jesse has made a fascinating collection of plastic artefacts of the period.

A German art historian once said, 'One can learn as much about a civilization from a shoe as from a cathedral.' I think one can go further, and suggest that the *kitsch* or inferior or tasteless objects from any given period have *more* to tell us about that period than the works of individual genius. By definition, the great works were produced by exceptional men and women, people who rose above the level of their contemporaries. But what of the ordinary people: what did they want in their houses? What pictures did they hang (or paint) on their walls? The interest of Pompeii is that the lava petrified a town something like Chelmsford, with no metropolitan elegance or exorbitant luxury. We get far more idea of normal life in the Roman Empire from it than from the Arch of Constantine in Rome, or from the fine statues in glass cases in the British Museum, monuments commissioned by noblemen and Caesars.

In 1976 I was co-organizer (with Mary Banham and Christopher Firmstone) of an exhibition at the Victoria and Albert Museum to celebrate the 25th anniversary of the Festival of Britain, 1951 ('A Tonic to the Nation'.) While trying to re-create the great South Bank exhibition which was produced by a coalition of the nation's top talents, we also devoted a large space to showing how ordinary people lived in the 1950s decade which *followed* the Festival. They did not live in Domes of Discovery or have Skylons in their gardens. Neither could many of them afford the Gordon Russell furniture on which the then Council of Industrial Design was so keen. Some of the orginal Festival designers, who came to the opening of the V & A show, reproached us bitterly for putting *kitsch* on display in the 1950s section, not only in a mock living room, but also in 'reconstructed' shops devoted to toys, clothes, books and magazines. I understood their feelings. They would have liked our exhibition to represent only the best of 1950s design, the things they were striving for when they masterminded the Festival. But one must remember that they were only a minute fraction of the public—and what a high-principled and specialist fraction. Ultimately their ideas did percolate down into everyday design, and the Festival had something to do with that; but it was often, as Sir Misha Black admitted, in a bastardized form. (In the same way, the ideals of Gropius and the Bauhaus were debased before the Second World War. Gropius complained of 'imitators who prostituted our fundamental concepts into modish trivialities.') So collectors of 1950s relics—and there are several already—also have a clear choice between 'quality' artefacts, such as Gerald Benney silver, and non-quality things like 'telly-tables' (which one clipped to the armchair and ate off while watching Gilbert Harding or 'The Grove Family'.) It would be a pity if either were lost to posterity.

Duff Cooper (consort of the immortal Diana) called his autobiography *Old Men Forget*. That is only too true, and so is the rider, that Young Men Remember. That is why I am glad that the Preston Polytechnic, at the beginning of 1980, staged an exhibition about the 1970s. Who, in twenty or even ten years' time, will remember that this was the age of Adidas bags, airbrush paintings, digital watches, Habitat and High-Tech, punk, platform shoes, patches, skateboards, streakers and skinheads? It is quite wrong to dismiss this early consideration of the period as simply a maundering or at any rate premature exercise in 'nostalgia'. It is history from the oven while the oven is still hot. The consciousness that 'the antique' is moving ever nearer our own day, inevitably leads to speculation as to what may be 'the antiques of the future'. Here, opinions differ even more violently than on antiques of the past. I was once on a television programme with Arthur Negus and others, for which everybody was asked to bring along his idea of 'antiques of the future', selecting things currently on the market. One participant brought what I thought was a beautiful cabinet, round-topped, of white wood with a brilliantly red-lacquered interior. Negus surveyed it scornfully. 'It looks like a Punch and Judy show, if you ask me,' he said. His own contribution was some varnished figures carved out of twigs and tree roots in the New Forest by a contemporary craftsman. The man who had brought the 'Punch and Judy' got his own back: 'They look like *plastic wood* to me,' he sniffed.

I would place high on any list of antiques of the future, the exquisite glass engravings of Laurence Whistler, the wood-engravings of Joan Hassall and Reynolds Stone (of whom the latter, I am proud to say, engraved my bookplate on wood just before his death last year) and the furniture of John Makepeace. They are all in the 'quality' category. In the 'social interest' category, I would go for children's toys. Because they are surrendered to destructive kiddies, these are terribly vulnerable and perishable: so the ones you save will automatically have rarity value. And toys reflect, perhaps better than any adult goods, the changes of the age. Moonmen and robots, Cindy-dolls and action-men, miniature weather-forecasting stations, scale models of cars, trains and aeroplanes, will all reveal to future collectors our curious preoccupations.

People who like this sort of thing
will find this the sort of thing they like

Abraham Lincoln
1809 – 1865

Introduction

When the first ape climbed down from its tree and shambled along the ground it was setting a fashion. And when another ape plopped down beside the first it was following that fashion. We, their descendants, have been setting and following fashions ever since. It is the purpose of this book to assess the present state of fashion in antiques and other items which people collect.

THERE has probably never been a greater interest in these matters than exists now, and the reasons are not far to seek. It is a charming, if sometimes maddening, human characteristic to consider that things ain't what they used to be, so we are thereby naturally inclined to like things about which we can wistfully say 'they don't make them like that nowadays.' There are enough of us saying it to drown the aberrant voices adding 'and a good thing too.' In fact there are so many people hunting antiques that fashions in such things are changing very swiftly. It is a crashingly obvious truth that there can never be any more antiques, and that every one destroyed—by worm or fire or whatever—reduces the supply which, in turn, increases the demand. But, like all crashingly obvious truths, it is slightly misleading. While the total number of antiques in existence can only decrease, the number in circulation at any one time can be widely different from that a decade or a year or day earlier or later. Every time a collection comes on the market there is a test of the state of fashion. Items which have previously been out of circulation present themselves for public approval just like any other animal, vegetable or mineral in the market place. In his attempts to attract approval the seller is trying to influence fashion.

It follows, therefore, that if he is successful the public will be hungry for more, and will eagerly gobble up every similar item which comes on the market. If he is not successful in drumming up enthusiasm the public will greet the similar item with a weary sigh of 'oh no, not another of those', and turn away. The item, however worthy, is out of fashion.

Fashion may really be likened to a pond. If a man standing on one side throws in a stone the consequent ripples may wet the feet of a man standing on the other. The big splash is in the middle but people far away are ultimately affected by it. It only needs two rich-rich collectors to want the same thing for the price to soar. And a huge price paid in one place will influence prices far away from the great throbbing heart of things. A country dealer with a humbler example of the same type may be persuaded to dust it off, stick a new price tag on it and place it prominently in the window. A passer-by will notice it, see the price and immediately assume that the item must have some merit which he has not previously noticed. Quite possibly it has such merit. Once our attention is drawn to something we look at it and discover all sorts of virtues which we have not bothered to observe before. Thus a fashion which has been artificially created may well survive because it is based on genuine quality.

Some of the dottier fashions, on the other hand, soon peter out because they are not worth sustaining. The *Incroyables,* for instance, wore breeches so tight that they could not sit down, and they may even have envied the freedom of movement of the *Sans Culottes* who had no breeches at all to impede them. It is small wonder that this absurd fashion came to an end which would have been abrupt even without the help of the guillotine. It may be that a fashion of our own time will quickly disappear when popstars come to realise that tinted glasses do not actually assist vision on a dark night.

But things which have become popular because of their acknowledged merit tend to stay if not in the spotlight of fashion at least still somewhere on the stage. In the early days their appeal seems to be accentuated just because they have previously been derided. No doubt the primitive apes, swinging gracefully from branch to branch, poured scorn and other droppings on their pioneering brothers shambling along the forest floor. Equally the earthbound apes, in their turn, must have poked fun at their own offspring rearing ridiculously up to walk on their hind legs.

It is notorious that people are slow to recognise genius but once recognition comes it is seldom withdrawn again. Turner, Picasso and Henry Moore are examples. The same principle applies to fashions in style as to individual artists. It is only about a hundred years since the Victorians, intoxicated with admiration of their own achievements, considered that 18th century furniture was old-fashioned stuff with nothing to recommend it. When a few perceptive folk began to bring it down from the attics its quality became apparent to anybody who bothered to look at it, and it has been appreciated—and itself appreciated—ever since. But for the first half of this century almost nobody except Queen Mary took any notice of Regency styles. Then, during the Second World War, some enterprising dealers bought up all the Regency furniture they could find, and at rock bottom prices. It escaped the bombing and in due course they launched it on the market with great skill. The rich glowing colours of the rosewood, the brass inlay, the flamboyance of the dolphins and the brightness of the stripes made an instant appeal to a generation starved of luxury by the drabness of war. It was a fashion artificially created but it has lasted because it was based on sound quality.

In the natural cycle of action and reaction everything Victorian was pushed into limbo and has only recently emerged. Victorian furniture, silver and paintings will probably never again be neglected, for the fineness of the craftsmanship of the first two outweighs any floridness of design, and the pictures, particularly landscapes, can stand comparison with earlier schools.

Fifty years ago, when the Grosvenor House Antique Dealers Fair was founded, an arbitrary minimum age-limit of a hundred years was set for the qualification 'antique'. But the pace has quickened since then, and collectors are turning their attention to things made in or just before their own lifetimes. The 'unconsidered trifles' of yesterday are the fashionable items of today, and crazes of the day before are as dead as, if not the dodo, at least the yo-yo.

The present time, then, is an appropriate moment to survey the scene, to assess the strength and weakness of trends in fashion. It is, however, far from our intention to suggest that it is desirable to acquire something solely because other people like it. Rather, we want to draw the reader's attention to something which he may not have noticed for himself, in the hope that he will make up his own mind. We do not sneer at the man who says 'I don't know anything about Art but I know what I like.' We applaud his sturdy individuality. Trends and fashion pass him by. They swirl round the rock of his independence and leave it unmoved. But if we can help him to see what other people like, and why, so much the better.

For the most part we demonstrate the ebb and flow of fashion by giving examples of prevalent prices and, as a convenient yardstick, we refer mostly to prices obtained at one or other of the main auction houses. But this should not be taken as a recommendation that purchases be made only at auction. A collector has to be very sure of what he is doing before he competes with expert dealers, and a cheap price usually means a bad bargain. Prices in shops are generally higher and worth it. The dealer may need to do some restoration which is expensive, he may lock up capital in any particular item for longer than he had intended, he has his profit and his overheads to consider. On the other hand buying something at auction is fun. As Oscar Wilde said about something quite other, it is like feasting with tigers, the danger is half the excitement.

But if you prefer to play safe look out for a dealer with a sound reputation who shows the sign of the British Antique Dealers' Association in his window and a smile on his honest face.

Douglas J K Wright Ltd.

Oriental Art

A very fine Arita bottle of pear shape tapering towards a near-cylindrical neck with everted rim, painted in underglaze-blue with a wide band showing a flowering shrub beneath a narrow band of lobe design, the neck with a band of stylised leaves beneath a 'comb' design. Third quarter 17th century. Japanese. 38.4cm. high.

34 CURZON STREET, LONDON, W1Y 7AE

Telephone: 01-629 9993/4

Plate I. An extremely fine Baluch long rug, possibly from the Herat area of Afghanistan rather than Persia. 17th century.

CHAPTER ONE

Oriental Carpets and their Market

by Ian Bennett

. . . carpet dusting, though a pretty trade
Is not the imperative labour after all,

Elizabeth Barrett Browning
1806 – 1861

IF ART dealers in general are looked upon with a considerable amount of suspicion by the public, then Oriental carpet dealers must be the subjects of the greatest opprobrium. Certainly when I began to collect carpets seriously about three years ago, having been writing about them for considerably longer than that, I was more than a little nervous, so mesmerised was I by horrendous tales of the deep villainy rife in the carpet world, I was, therefore, somewhat surprised to discover that, quite contrary to my prejudices, carpet dealers are an extremely friendly, knowledgeable and reliable group who take great interest in the things they sell and, monetary considerations apart, are pleased to help a new collector simply for the pleasure of having been instrumental in the formation of what both they and the collector himself hope will turn into a collection of rugs of more than passing interest. I say all this at the outset simply because the first question I am asked over and over again by people wishing to collect Oriental carpets, or just to buy one or two examples as decorative features in their homes, has to do with the honesty of the carpet trade.

If this is the greatest worry, then a close second is the despair many people have about ever being able to understand, let alone master, what they see as the hideous complexities of the subject. There are so many types, some of them differing only slightly one from another, and so many other added difficulties, such as fineness of weave, type of knotting, age, the presence or absence of synthetic dyes, etc., that many would-be collectors are put off by a task which they consider altogether too daunting. Again, the problems are, I believe, greatly exaggerated.

Carpets can be divided into three very broad categories: 1, Classical carpets, that is pieces assumed to have been made before 1800 AD; 2, tribal and village rugs, which, in terms of those examples worth serious collecting interest, date in the main from

1. East Turkestan carpet attributed to the region of Khotan. 2nd half of 17th century.

2. Turkish village rug from the Konya region. 2nd half of 17th century.

the end of the 18th to the beginning of the 20th centuries. Examples are, of course, still being woven today, although the quality of such things declined rapidly after about 1920, since when very few pieces worth collecting have been made; finally 3, which consists of commercially produced town carpets made, in general, in large factories. The bulk of this market is made up of Persian rugs, which have been made under these conditions since about the middle of the 19th century and are still being made today (recent political events in Iran have almost ended production—certainly a total embargo has been placed on exports).

These broad categories having been established, there are obviously very many smaller sub-categories within them. Today, the greatest collecting interest is focused on the second of our three groups, tribal and village rugs. The reasons for this are easy enough to establish—they are available in great numbers; there is a very wide diversity of type and quality; and the price range is extremely wide, from under £100 to around £30,000, thus enabling just about every interested party to buy something. One might add—and this is perhaps the most crucial point—that tribal and village rugs probably offer the best value for money; if one knows what one is doing, it is still possible to buy something of real quality and interest, something which also stands a very good chance of being an extremely profitable investment, for under £250. The same cannot be said of either the first or third categories.

There are, basically, two ways of buying Oriental carpets, or, for that matter, most other kinds of art—either at auction or from a dealer. Not surprisingly, the one avenue is always trying to promote itself at the expense of the other, and many people become a little confused, not to mention annoyed, by the charges

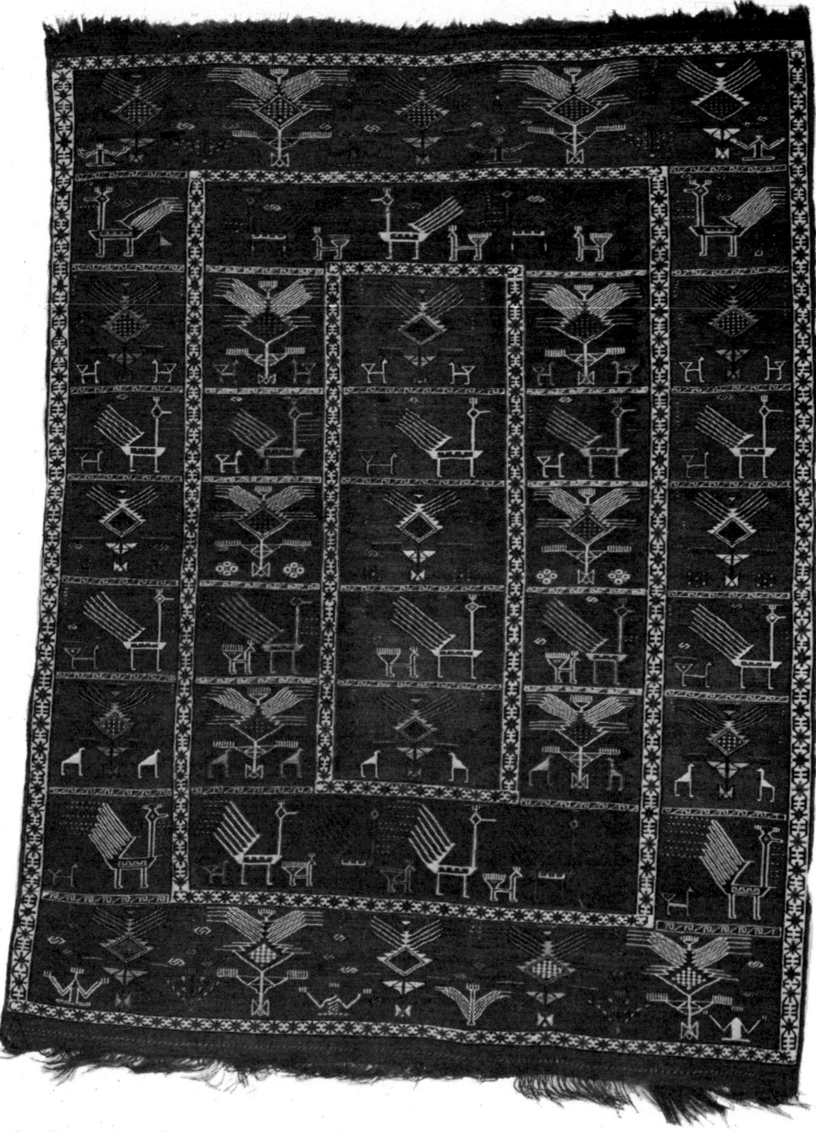

3. Caucasian flat-woven rug of the late 19th or early 20th century.

and counter-charges that are constantly being laid.

For the inexperienced buyer, Oriental carpets have their own special problems and both the auction houses and the dealers have their own built-in disadvantages. As a beginner, however, I think it has to be accepted that you must take a certain amount on trust and it is very probable, some people would say inevitable, that you are going to make a few mistakes to start with.

The first thing to be realised about carpets—something which is, admittedly, somewhat subjective and a little difficult to define absolutely—is that they can be both works of art and functional objects, something which defines the 'applied arts' in general and separates them from the so-called 'fine arts', which have no function. However, in the case of rugs, the majority of examples, although perfectly functional, have little, if any, claim on the title 'work of art'. Thus the rugs which are offered in the carpet departments of major stores—the sorts of rugs which may be labelled 'Pakistani Bokhara', 'Golden Afghan' or 'super-washed Chinese'—have absolutely no artistic significance, yet are perfectly good functional objects. They can be extremely expensive, however, although it is probably true that the better quality examples, if treated with great care (something which, admittedly, rather obviates their functional purpose) will probably hold their value; some, such as the finest Persian carpets, may even increase in value, especially if rug production there does not return to normal levels for some years, as seems likely.

It is obvious that the serious collector of Oriental rugs would not be interested in such things and, in the long term, it is the growth of a strong private collecting sector which creates and supports a strong market. Thus the beginner has to learn to distinguish between what, in the trade, are known as 'furnishing pieces' and those examples which might be described by the ghastly expression 'collectors' pieces', those rugs, in other words, which have some claim on the title 'work of art'. Naturally, there is

4. Mongolian woven saddle-rug, probably of mid-19th century.

some degree of overlap, especially among pieces made early this century; these, while tending towards commercialism, still retain elements of a genuine tribal or village tradition; and, of course, there is also a certain amount of disagreement over some examples.

Obviously, the greater the knowledge of both buyer and seller, the less likelihood there is of disagreements. However, in London, there are only very few real experts in tribal and village rugs, the majority of dealers concentrating on our third category and only buying examples of the second when they are 'furnishing pieces' (although very often the dealer cannot tell the difference between a genuine old tribal carpet and more modern commercial examples). It should be added that this same degree of unawareness extends to the salerooms, who will often catalogue a rug in a way which suggests that it is a superb example of tribal weaving when in fact it is a late and purely decorative furnishing piece; this is not done, I hasten to add, with any mendacity or with any intent to deceive but, generally speaking, simply out of ignorance.

This problem of interpretation does not apply to our third category. However, it is probably true to say that few people 'collect' Persian city rugs as works of art; their main market is with rich individuals furnishing their homes in somewhat lavish taste. The best examples, dating from the second half of the 19th century (many dealers and auction houses persist in cataloguing some examples as having been made in the first half of the 19th century, although there is no evidence for this and very strong evidence that the manufacture of such pieces did not begin until the end of the 1850s at the very earliest) are extremely expensive, especially if they are in good condition and more especially if they are woven in silk rather than wool. Admittedly, the strongest buyers over the last two or three years have been Iranian dealers and rich private collectors from the same country and there is some evidence that the market has fallen slightly since the revolution. Many rich Iranians put a lot of their money into carpets before fleeing the country and have been surprised, not to say dismayed, to find that the price level for newish Persian rugs is lower in the West than it is (or was) in Iran.

Our first category, Classical carpets, has its own problems. The primary one, of course, is availability. Although there is a surprisingly high number of Classical pieces offered for sale every year—the majority, it seems, coming through the auction houses —many examples, especially if they are very large and very worn, are of remarkably little value; indeed, many are worth more if cut into fragments and sold as such, than if they are marketed in one piece!

This leads on to the second problem, which is the very subjective one of quality. There is a vast price difference between what is by general consent a great early example of a given type,

5. 17th century prayer rug made in the south west Caucasus.

and a late, decadent, example. And another point worth noting is that a good early piece in terrible condition can often be worth considerably more than a late piece in almost mint condition, (this can also be true of tribal and village rugs, although buyers tend to be less discriminating in these markets, especially in such countries as Germany where condition seems to be the paramount criterion for measuring 'worth', a somewhat illogical state of affairs).

The third major problem with Classical carpets concerns fakes. There are very many marvellously clever late 19th and early 20th century fakes of classical carpets; the use of the word 'fake' in this context may be slightly over-emotive, as it is probable that many of them were not made with intention of deceiving gullible buyers into thinking that they were purchasing genuine old rugs but were

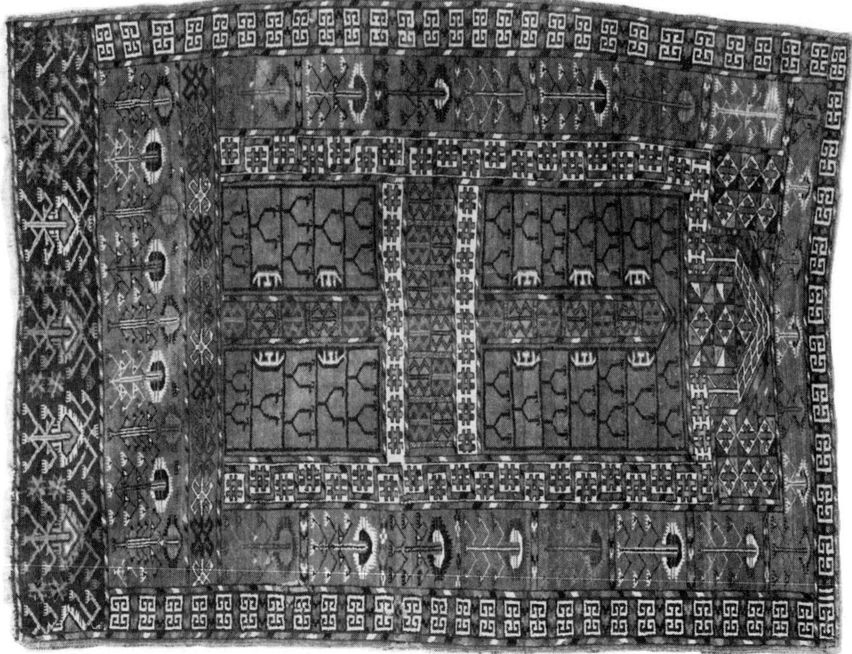

6. An 'Ensi'. Not a prayer-rug but a hanging for covering the entrance of a tent of nomadic Turkoman tribes.

made as admitted copies either for collectors or simply as furnishing pieces; others, such as the famous 'Salting' group, were produced in the 19th century Ottoman Court workshops in a style adapted from Safavid Persian weaving styles, simply because the Turkish nobility considered this style to be the most suited to the sumptuous silk and gold and silver thread carpets they liked so much. The fact that early Western dealers and scholars could not tell the difference between these and real Safavid carpets can hardly be blamed on the Turks (many Western 'experts', it is obvious, still cannot tell them apart).

However, whether made to deceive or not, fakes and copies have been abused consistently by Western dealers and auction houses, generally because they have not had the expertise to spot them. The 'Salting' group, named after a carpet given to the Victoria and Albert Museum by Sir George Salting, was accepted as genuine by most scholars for many years, an acceptance which was, of course, followed by the carpet trade. Similarly, copies of predominantly Turkish carpets made in this century at the Tuduc factory in Romania have been the cause of immense problems. They are so superbly made that examples are still accepted as genuine. The late Professor Kurt Erdmann, one of the greatest scholars Oriental carpet studies have produced, wrote a famous essay called 'A Carpet unmasked', which was included in his posthumous collection of essays, *Seven Hundred Years of Oriental Carpets*. In this, he exposed the existence in several of the world's leading museums of 20th century copies purporting to be genuine 17th century products. He remarked that proper care and attention to detail would soon weed out the copies from the genuine rugs and, as if to prove his point, illustrated what he considered to be a genuine example of one of the most copied groups, a white-ground 'Chintamani' pattern carpet supposed to have been made in the 17th century in the Turkish city of Ushak; unfortunately, this example, in the Berlin Museum, and illustrated in colour in Erdmann's book, is itself a Tuduc copy!

With classical carpets, as with later tribal and village rugs, it is absolutely essential to get expert advice before embarking on a collection or even before buying one or two pieces for the home; mistakes can be extremely costly. The major salerooms offer free advice (well, it actually costs 10% of the hammer price) to prospective purchasers and the attitude of many of them to tribal pieces is, on the whole, comparative lack of interest compounded by ignorance; this means, of course, that the carpet collector with some expertise can still pick up real bargains, even in the major London auction rooms. Such an attitude, I should add, does not exist in the few specialist carpet auction houses.

A good dealer will tell a prospective client everything about the condition of a rug in his stock and will also offer, to the best of his knowledge, advice about the piece's age, condition and quality. The accuracy of this information depends on the expertise of the dealer and since there are comparatively few dealers who can claim genuine expertise on tribal and village rugs and even fewer who know much about Classical carpets, it is almost as important to choose one's dealer with care as it is to choose one's rug.

I should add that the best specialist dealers will often charge more for a rug than a non-specialist dealer (just as tribal and village rugs tend to fetch more in a sale held by a specialist carpet auctioneer than in a sale held by one of the general auctioneers). This is because the specialist carpet dealer will have a greater awareness of a particular rug's age, quality, rarity and importance; he will *pay* more for good examples than will the non-specialist dealer and thus will *charge* more. Also, he is dealing with a clientele who, in general, are as knowledgeable as he. My view is that it is acceptable to pay more for a piece under these circumstances because, as a beginner, one will not have any nagging doubts; at least one will be confident that one has purchased a rug of real quality and distinction, the sort of piece which, in the long term, stands the best chance of being a really good investment as well as affording one the greatest pleasure to own.

Colour plate and Figures 1–5 by courtesy of Christie's. Figure 6 by courtesy of Sotheby's.

Pair of Sheffield Plate Wine Coolers by Matthew Bolton.
Sold on 28th March, 1980. £950

GALERIE 1900
267 CAMDEN HIGH STREET NW1 485 1001

An Investment in Beauty..
two thousand years ago, the
world has seldom seen the beauty of
nature so perfectly expressed as in
the birds, animals and flowers of
Boehm of Malvern England and
Trenton, U.S.A.
Meticulous attention to detail in every
Boehm study ensures lasting visual
and aesthetic pleasure and
investment potential.
Boehm sculptures in both open and
limited editions are much sought
after by collectors and are
represented in over ninety museums
and art centres throughout the
world.
Elizabeth of Glamis Rose Limited
Edition issued in honour of Her
Majesty Queen Elizabeth The
Queen Mother.
You are invited to visit our Malvern Showroom,
between 10am-5pm Monday to Friday.
Please write or telephone for full
details and list of stockists.
BOEHM
Boehm of Malvern England Ltd., Tanhouse Lane, Malvern WR14 1LG, England.
Telephone: Leigh Sinton (0886) 32111. Telex: 338759.
Boehm Porcelain Gallery, 225 Fifth Avenue, Suite 104, New York 10010 U.S.A.
Telephone: 212-679-2861

1. Bow vase and cover, circa 1750. it sold for £1,500 in October 1979.

CHAPTER TWO
English and Continental Ceramics
by Barbara Wedgwood

There's a pleasure eternally new,
'Tis to gloat on the glaze and the mark
Of china that's ancient and blue.

Andrew Lang
1844 – 1912

"OLD china is below nobody's taste, since it has been the Duke of Argyll's, whose understanding has never been doubted either by his friends or enemies," proclaimed that tireless letter writer Lady Mary Wortley Montagu two and a half centuries ago, when the age of the great china collections was just commencing.

Of course pottery had been known to the world almost from the beginning of time, but the making of porcelain only began in China in the ninth century—which is why its common name has always been china. Harder, thinner and more vitreous than other ceramics, its secret lay in the special clay with which it was made, kaolin.

During the Middle Ages a few pieces of china came into Europe where the inhabitants, according to their status, ate off silver, pewter, wooden trenchers or crude peasant pottery. In the seventeenth century the Dutch at Delft made some excellent imitations of china in pottery, but their ware lacked the whiteness and the shining glaze of porcelain. By the end of the seventeenth century the obsession for true china became a European mania. The holds of ships of the East India Company were crammed with it. Alchemists sought the secret of transforming pottery into porcelain just as they sought to turn base metal into gold.

Only at the beginning of the eighteenth century was the formula for porcelain discovered in Europe by Johann Böttger at Meissen under the patronage of Augustus the Strong, Elector of Saxony. A true collector and a man of strong passions, Augustus sired over three hundred and fifty illegitimate children. Equally as enthusiastic and generous in the decorative as in the amorous arts, he demanded that his craftsmen experiment with a wide variety of materials, models and decorations. Most items with the famous crossed swords back-stamp were painted in the Meissen factory by skilled artists; however, unfinished or imperfect pieces were

Plate II. Meissen vase and cover, circa 1730. It fetched £3,000 in November 1979.

sometimes sold or given to local peasants who decorated the items themselves and established a thriving *hausmaler* or cottage industry. Hence, the charm, quantity and variety of Meissen which, two hundred and seventy years after its establishment is, unlike its virile founder, still going strong.

For well over half of the eighteenth century Meissen (commonly called Dresden) had a monopoly on the market. No aristocratic dining room on the Continent or in England was complete without a dish, a set of vases, a collection of figures or a dessert set of Meissen. Secrets, however, are seldom kept when the rewards of betrayal are sufficiently lucrative. By 1770 there were successful factories at Vienna, Strasbourg, Frankenthal and Nymphenburg. In France, Louis XV, the arbiter of European fashion, gave the royal *imprimateur* (a double interlaced L) to his magnificent and costly factory, first called Vincennes, then in 1757, Sèvres. The ware first produced was soft-paste porcelain, beautiful in designs and range of colours but technically inferior to Meissen. It was popularised by Louis XV's glamorous mistress Madame de Pompadour after whom the famous Sèvres pink, made only for a few years, was named. Unlike the figures, vases and decorative garniture of Meissen, the glory of Sèvres lay in its tableware. Chantilly, St Cloud and Mennecy, who used gold in profusion, produced better quality porcelain but never rivalled Sèvres in commercial success.

In England the development of soft-paste porcelain occured at about the same time at Derby, Chelsea, Bow, Coalport, Swansea and Worcester. True bone china, which distinguishes English from Continental porcelain, was not achieved until 1796 by Josiah Spode. The crude terra cotta pottery of seventeenth century Staffordshire (a place used generically for the pottery industry, like Dresden, or in France, Limoges) and the salt-glazed wares of the early eighteenth century generally have a rustic charm more appealing than their Continental counterparts, though today such items as a Ralph Toft slipware charger dated 1669 or a Whieldon agate teapot of 1750 are more likely to be found on the shelves of a museum than on the shelves of a private collector.

English sophistication in taste, as in technique, lagged behind the Continent throughout the eighteenth century with the single exception of the most celebrated of all potters, Josiah Wedgwood. No one man before him or since realised both the possibilities and the limitations of the material and at the same time stamped it with his own unmistakable and remarkable style. The lavish, exuberant rococco style to which Meissen and Sèvres were so superbly suited gave way to the neo-classicism which Wedgwood, with the new techniques of mass production, was exceptionally adept.

Wedgwood's creamware was thought to rival china in beauty and, most importantly, was much cheaper. By the end of the eighteenth century the modellers and painters at Meissen and

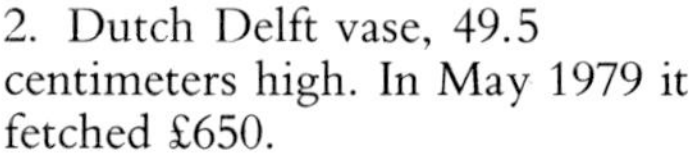

2. Dutch Delft vase, 49.5 centimeters high. In May 1979 it fetched £650.

3. Worcester tankard with square mark of the First Period. It sold for £850 in November 1978.

Sèvres, as well as at lesser Continental and English factories, were slavishly copying Wedgwood. In 1810 a disgruntled young English aristocrat making the obligatory tour of the Continent complained that in all of France there was not an inn that did not serve its meals off Wedgwood.

Throughout the nineteenth century the craze for china and creamware reached epidemic proportions. Colossal dinnerware services, toilet sets, spittoons, gigantic vases, miniatures, figures, thimbles, door handles, candlesticks, pastille burners, jewellery, scent bottles, dairy pans, Toby Jugs and tablets for paintings–all were status symbols assiduously acquired. As ordinary people naturally accumulated more objects than knowledge, forgeries and fraud were inevitable. In 1891 the McKinley Tariff Act decreed that all objects imported into the United States had to be marked with their country of origin and thus provided a reliable guide to identifying and dating ceramics. Though pottery and porcelain not destined for the American market was not necessarily backstamped England or France or Germany, it was generally more practical to stamp or impress the country along with the factory's name or trademark. Fortunately also in the instance of pottery and porcelain, the mark was usually applied prior to the final firing and thus not easily removed. Collectors know that any china marked with the name of the country in which it was made is less than a hundred years old and therefore not an antique, though it may indeed be a work of art and worth considerably more than some items which *are* old but plentiful and inferior in quality and design.

According to the annual turnover figures released recently by the four leading London auction houses, the antique pottery and porcelain business is booming. Such figures as related to the market as a whole are, however, misleading. While specialist dealers and investment collectors have purchased rare and expensive items as a hedge against inflation, middle-priced items have not increased proportionately. In an effort to keep pace with inflation or at least to maintain market prices, dealers have tended to hold on to stock rather than to turn it over rapidly. On the whole, due to higher VAT, a stronger pound, increased interest rates and fewer overseas tourists, the retail business has been sluggish. Chipped, cracked, restored, ordinary and medium quality pieces are not selling, though these might well be wise purchases for the non-specialist in search of something attractive to place in a cabinet.

Perhaps because there were fewer foreign visitors in 1979 and because English buyers have a strong preference for their own factories, English pottery and porcelain in mint condition has remained the strongest category in ceramics. *Chelsea,* which is becoming comparatively scarce, is in good demand by collectors who are willing to pay prices in the range of £600 to £3,000 for unusual "gold anchor" and "raised anchor" plates and decorative items. *Bow,* which is equally scarce and much less expensive, appeals only to a limited circle of buyers and experiences little movement. A Bow plate may sell at auction for as little as £50 whereas the familar Bow recumbent pug dogs sell anywhere from £100 to £500. *Derby* fluctuates widely in both price and demand but is realizing a renewed interest, particularly in early nineteenth century botanical patterns and in figures which on average range at auction from £200 to £800.

Worcester, another English porcelain factory dating back to the eighteenth century, appears endlessly plentiful in sale rooms and shops. Small items in blue and white, such as pickle dishes and creamers, are in particular favour now and are bringing anywhere from £50 to £300. Worcester patterns with flowers and birds and stamped with the open crescent mark are also in fashion. More than any other English porcelain factory, Worcester demonstrates the widest range in price for items in good condition. At Christie's auction of November 1979, estimates of Dr. Wall cups and saucers extended from £130-£150 for a well-known Oriental design to £1,000-£1,200 for a chrysanthemum pattern with green diaper border.

The demand for *Staffordshire figures* has declined recently, and auction prices, on the whole, have been disappointing for the auctioneer. On October 9 at Christie's South Kensington, part of the fine Kimpton Collection was sold at prices ranging from £20 to

4. Wedgwood black basalt vase. In February 1979 it fetched £900.

£950 for a rare group of The Victory, modelled as an English sailor with a Turkish and a French soldier.

Royal Doulton figures and Toby Jugs, which again appeal only to a particular but loyal market, frequently come under the hammer at South Kensington or Belgravia for less than £50. *Early Staffordshire Toby Jugs* are likely to bring ten times that amount.

Wedgwood, the most popular of all factories in the American market, has maintained its desirability in the various categories of creamware, china, jasper, basalt and lustre. Demand for the rarer and finer pieces exceeds supply. Prices rose sharply as fewer pieces came up for auction in 1979 than in recent years. If there is an excess of Derby and Worcester both in the shops and in the sale rooms, there is a discernable shortage of Wedgwood. Eighteenth century jasper, first period china (made only between 1812 and 1822) and wide bordered coloured groundlay plates of the 1810 to

5. A pair of Mettlach polychrome vases which sold for £350 in October 1979.

1820 period have been in particular favour, if in mint condition. Prices on eighteenth century jasper and basalt have ranged from £80 for a portrait medallion to £4,000 for a large Wedgwood & Bentley plaque. A thirty-two piece tea service in first period china sold in October 1979 at Christie's for £1,000. A 1930s Skeaping figure of a seal sold at Sotheby's Belgravia for £65. Though prices on fairyland lustre, designed by Daisy Makeig-Jones in the 1920s, still remain high, interest in lustreware in general, as in the rarer colours of twentieth century jasper, appears to be waning. At Bonham's in September, a Wedgwood fairyland lustre bowl sold for £500 whereas at Sotheby's Belgravia a Wedgwood butterfly lustre bowl of the same size and quality sold for £60. Early Wedgwood creamware is a highly sophisticated taste and consistently remains undervalued except for wares decorated by David Rhodes or the early prints of Sadler and Green.

Whether made by Wedgwood or by other English factories, *Commemorative wares* of all periods have lost interest and declined in price. Possibly the market has been glutted by recent editions which have tended to detract from the old. Also, the decorations, both old and new, have generally been in painfully bad taste. Pot

6. The large Worcester vase of 1903 fetched £780 in October 1979. The smaller pair, also Worcester, and made in 1920, fetched £350 in the same sale.

lids and cottage pastille burners, inexpensive fields for collecting, are no longer as sought after as in the past. There is less interest, too, in the broad area of Victoriana, in majolica and in parian ware, except for items made by *Wedgwood* or *Minton*.

There is little or no retail activity with other English factories, such as *Liverpool, Spode, Coalport, Mason, New Hall Adams or Nantgarw,* possibly reflecting the view that they are localised tastes and have little interest for foreigners.

Among foreign factories, the strength, as always, is in *Meissen,* which continues to dominate the market. English collectors are relatively few; the major buyers come from the Continent and the

United States. Prices are high. At Sotheby's on November 27 a superb collection of ninety-one lots of early Meissen, dating from 1715-1760, was sold at prices ranging from £340 to £14,000. An especially fine pear-shaped teapot, circa 1725, realised £3,400. At Christie's sale in September 1979 at North Mymms Park near Hatfield in Hertfordshire, a two hundred and five piece Meissen service with the Altar Gelber Loewe pattern, sold in twenty-six lots, totalled £93,410. At an auction held by Neale's of Nottingham, a nineteenth century group of water nymphs sold for £400 and a twentieth century rendition of Augustus and his wife made £220.

In contrast, *Sèvres* is unpredictable. Eighteenth century wares are currently at a standstill, probably because of the lack of Continental buyers. *Mennecy, Chantilly* and *St Cloud* show little activity and are underpriced. On the other hand, *Capo di Monti* and *Doccia* are rare and high priced.

Both *Delft* and *English Delft* preferred mainly by Dutch and German customers, are keeping pace with the general upward trend in prices. Tiles remain in strong demand. Blue printed wares from both English and Continental factories maintain their popularity, are plentiful and inexpensive.

As Lady Mary Wortley Montagu correctly observed; "Old china is below nobody's taste"—but the taste for the 1980s is likely to be opportunistic, conservative and eclectic.

Colour plate and Figures 2, 3 and 4 by courtesy of Phillips. Figure 1 by courtesy of Sotheby's. Figures 5 and 6 by courtesy of Bonham's.

OFFICES ALSO AT BIRMINGHAM

LONDON BANBURY & SHIPSTON.

Fine Art Auctioneers and Valuers

Regular sales of Period furniture, works of art, ceramics, metalware, coins and stamps, collectors items and militaria, silver, jewellery and objects D'vertu, vintage wine, oil paintings, watercolours, drawings, prints and engravings (catalogues for all sales on subscription)

VALUATIONS AND INVENTORIES prepared in detail for Insurance, Probate, Family Division and Tax purposes.

No Buyers Premium *Modern Saleroom*

James II Walnut Chest £2400

The Old School, Tiddington,
Stratford-upon-Avon, CV37 7AW.

Tel: 0789-69415

1. Coffee pot by Thomas Holland, 1715. May 1979, £3,000.

CHAPTER THREE
Silver
by John K. D. Cooper

Bell, book and candle shall not drive me back,
when gold and silver becks me to come on.

William Shakespeare
1564 – 1616

SILVER is one of the most attractive metals, both to work and to possess. Unlike gold, whose heavy brilliance is tainted now more than ever by its intrinsic value and rarity, silver has a seductive warmth, a more subtle colour and feel than its costlier sister. In spite of its high price—£7.50+ per ounce in November 1979 as opposed to 30p in the 1950s—it remains as collectable as ever. The art is in knowing what to collect, where to find it and the criteria to apply in selecting the best examples.

The major restriction to be confronted with in buying silver is period. Anything of quality from before 1660, the date of the Restoration of King Charles II, will be out of range for 90% of collectors unless it be in the category of spoons or small boxes. Rarity, however, is still not enough. Quality demands the best possible state of preservation and the presence of a minimum number of hall marks. 16th century spoons, for example, which bear no marks at all, or merely a maker's or town mark suggesting an unknown provincial origin, can still be obtained for about £200 on average. At this price a spoon will be in somewhat worn condition, the edge of the bowl not too rubbed away, but the marks and any decoration clearly discernible if not very crisp. Those with a full tale of marks of London origin if very sharp, will now go for four figures each at the present rate of auction room record prices.

The unwary will fall back upon the controversial, and this fault applies in any period of collecting. This covers below average spoons, boxes and larger categories of plate where the condition is below average, the marks non-existent or unrecorded, the latter always giving rise to suspicion as a first reaction among most dealers, or where there is something else wrong.

'Wrongness' needs explanation, but something should first be said about the myth that hall marks are the be-all and end-all of

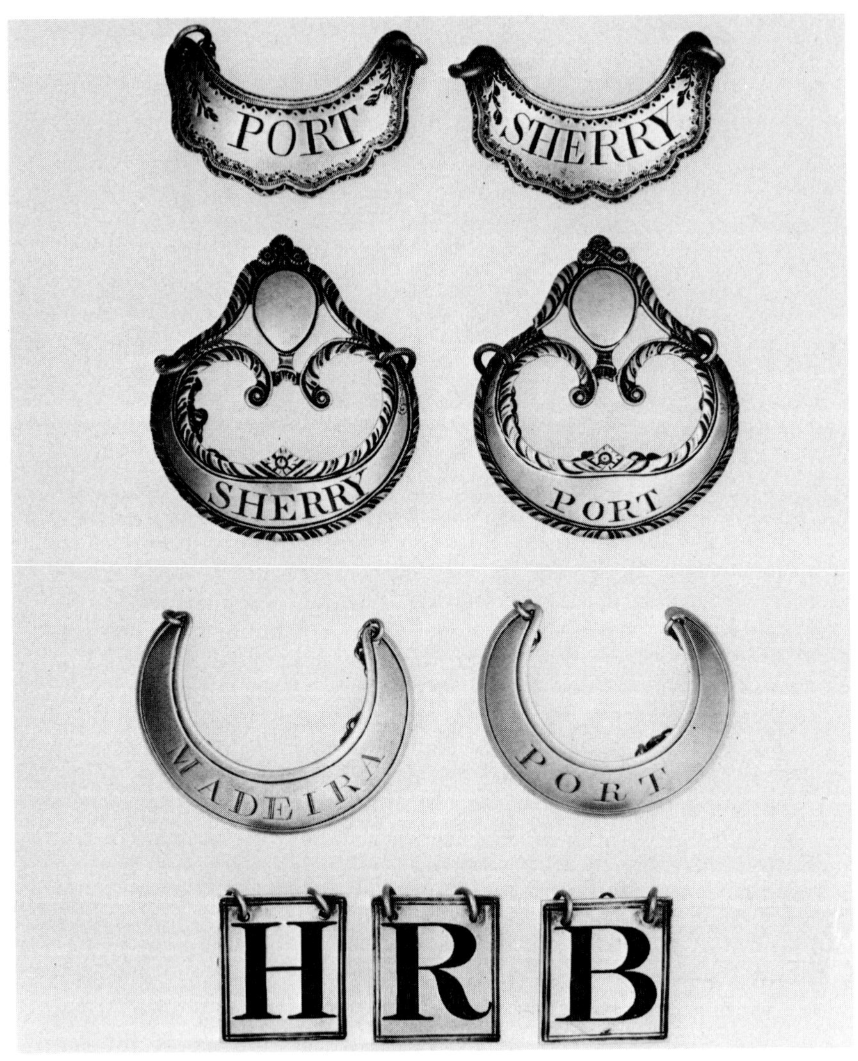

2. Wine labels. Top row, Perth mark., c. 1795, £110. Second row, Dublin circa 1785, £160. Third row, probably Irish, circa 1780, £190. All sold January 1979. Bottom row tablet letters for Hock, Brandy, and Rum. By James Atkins, 1807.

silver classification. They are not. Why were hallmarks introduced? A popular misconception is that they are applied for the benefit of future collectors! The truth is that they are marks of guarantee, one being used as a counter-check against the other, to assure the purchaser that metal used is of a certain purity. They have nothing to do with the actual quality of either design or manufacture whatever, as an inspection of any so-called

3. Teapot by Paul de Lamerie, 1714. February 1979, £3,800.

'silversmith's shop windows will testify.

The earliest English mark, the leopard's head, was introduced by the 'Mystery' or Company of Goldsmiths in London in 1300. It guaranteed that, according to 'touch' the standard of silver used was not less than ·925 pure, the 'sterling' standard still in use today. Not long after, in 1363, the maker's mark was added, mainly as a check on whose plate was whose at the time of assay.

The third mark, introduced in 1478, was the date letter, intended, as it still is, as a code to serve as a check upon the Assay Master himself in case of any infringement which might occur. The fourth mark, the lion passant, was introduced in 1544/5 as a further guarantee as to purity at a time when Henry VIII was flagrantly debasing the coinage by adding substantially more copper to it than the law allowed to help shore up his emptying coffers. As wrought plate up to that time obeyed the standard as coinage silver, the Goldsmiths' Company apparently initiated this mark to protect itself and the public from charges that it, too, might be marking debased silver. In the course of time, this mark became the English national standard and the leopard's head that representing London only.

Other marks any collector should learn to recognise and understand are the sovereign's head duty mark, introduced under George III in 1784 and used until 1890 to signify payment of an excise duty of sixpence in the ounce on silver of a certain minimum weight, supplemented by purely commemorative heads used for

Plate III. Digby Scott and Benjamin Smith the elder. A pair of sauceboats with covers and stands hallmarked 1806. Sold for £15,500 in October 1979.

the Silver Jubilee of King George V in 1935, the Coronation of our present Queen in 1953, and Her Majesty's Silver Jubilee in 1977.

Lastly, when the slightly higher 'Britannia' standard was introduced as a temporary measure to protect the newly refurbished coinage of William III's reign under the Wrought Plate Act of 1696, ·958 purity became compulsory and ·925 remained in use only for the coinage. The lion passant was replaced with the seated figure of Britannia and the leopard's head by a leopard's head erased (i.e. in profile). The inconvenience of mixing the purer alloy worked and the coinage increased accordingly, so that the Act was repealed in 1719. Silversmiths can still use the Britannia standard to this day if they wish. It occurs normally on reproduction plate of William III, Queen Anne and George I designs and can therefore cause confusion. This is where knowledge of the ever changing character and shape of marking punches is most useful in addition to knowing date letter codes. All collectors should note that the Dublin Assay Office has used a similar figure of Hibernia as a national mark since 1731—not to be confused with the figure of Britannia, who holds a shield, not an Irish harp.

No amount of written advice can compensate for the opportunity to learn from handling silver at an experienced dealer's or at a saleroom. It is there, 'in the field' so to speak, that lessons are learned, sometimes expensively through ignorance or bad memory. Patchings and repairs, sometimes cleverly disguised by plating over, removed armorial engravings leaving thin patches,

4. Vegetable dishes and covers by Paul Storr, 1835. May 1979, £3,700.

5. Pilgrim flask by Robert Garrard, 1876. September 1979, £5,800.

'improvements' achieved by adding or taking away decoration at different periods, tampering with handles and spouts, exchanging lids, over-polishing, transferring and tampering with hallmarks, blatant forgery—the pitfalls are many and various and quite equal to anything met with in furniture and ceramics. The best advice, apart from reading widely, is see and handle as much as possible, preferably in the company of an experienced collector or dealer. And it cannot be done in a hurry.

What is there to collect, then, in the disturbing economic climate of present time? Record prices have been bid at a recent substantial sale of English silver in London. For example, a Queen Anne rat-tail basting spoon of 1709 reached a little under £1,000, more than twice the expected price. From the late 17th century to about 1800, prices are bound to be reflected in this trend, unsavoury though it is for all but those who wish to sell. Sharply rising prices, however, should apply only to the rarest and finest pieces. The very wealthy collector is having to contend increasingly with the company investment portfolio and pieces are thus forced up steeply at the top end of the market.

The lessons of the late 1960s, when too many people lost their heads collecting all types of silver at ridiculous prices (for those days) must not be forgotten. With the production costs of modern silver at more than £10 per ounce, making probable retail price of a tea-spoon (of quality) around £15, collectors should be wary of going beyond a rate of £25 per ounce for anything made, say, since 1880, unless it is outstanding: that is, really good Art Nouveau, or Art Deco, or something in between such as Omar Ramsden. Unfortunately, many dealers will say the price per ounce guideline is 'old hat' and happily expect in excess of £40. Care must be exercised at this level. Not only must the condition and technical level be excellent, but the style should be really good of its period and the type of object be reasonably popular among collectors. It is no use buying the finest William IV egg épergne in existence, if there is little or no demand for that type of object.

The alternative is to look out for pieces which give you, the collector, the most pleasure, Admittedly, vinaigrettes, wine labels, tea caddy spoons and snuff boxes have always held large premiums over other types of small silver. Christening mugs, sets of knives, forks and spoons made for the same purpose, butter knives, fish servers and sugar tongs may have been dead weight among dealers over the last few decades, but as alternatives steadily price themselves out of the market selective buying of these categories could be both pleasurable and profitable.Spoons of various types and sizes have the advantage of being both useable, in most cases, and are rarely of displeasing design. Collecting different patterns from the 18th century onwards, remembering to concentrate on good condition and clear marks, affords considerable variety. If buying single pieces—there is a premium on the prices of pairs, fours or more—the price for a teaspoon should not exceed £8-£10, that for a dessert spoon £20-£30 and for a table spoon £25-£40 always, of course, depending upon bullion price fluctuations, V.A.T, and so forth. Unusual "double-struck" patterns (i.e. where a die has been used for striking both the upper and underneath design), such as the Coburg or popular King's Husk, are bound to cost more and pieces bearing George III or IV

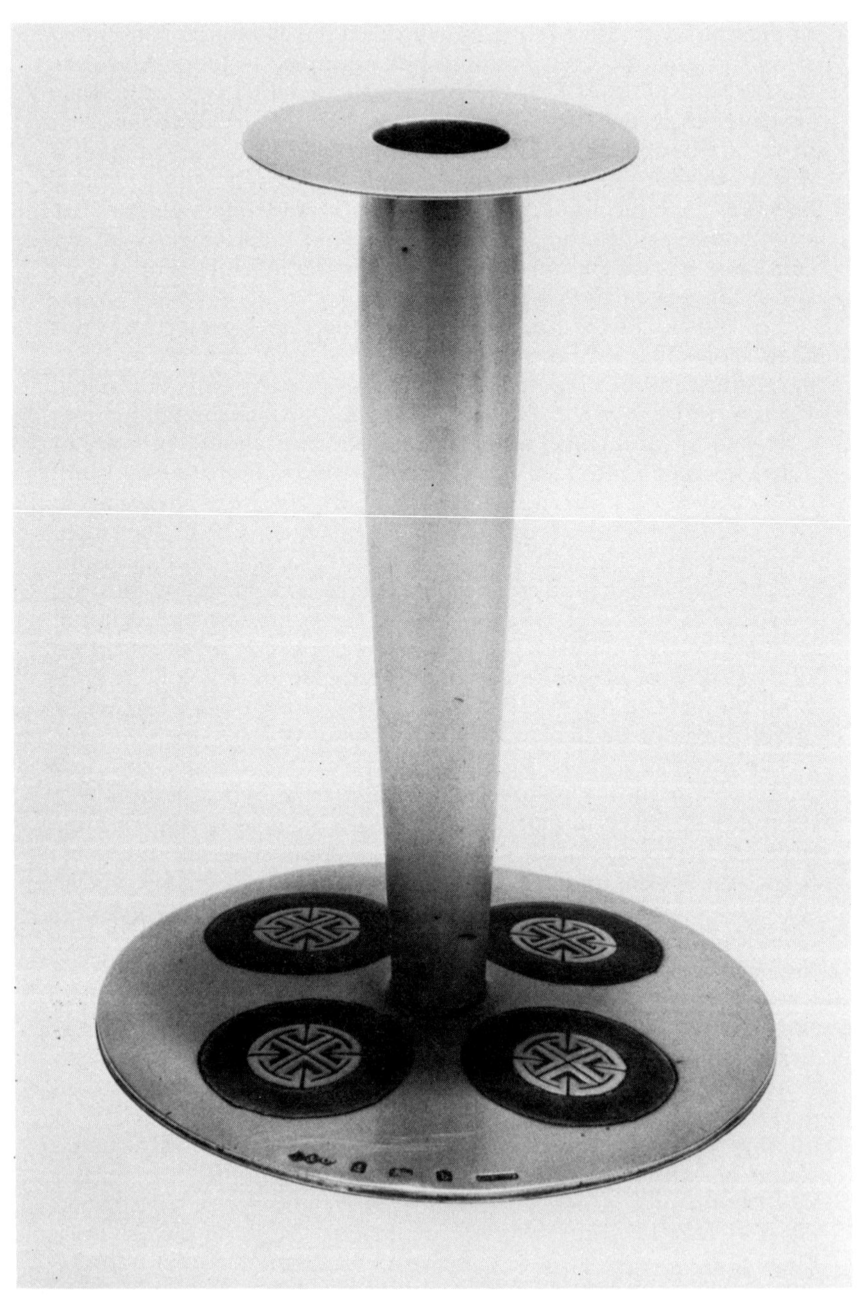

6. Silver and enamelled candlesticks by Liberty & Co, 1901. September 1979, £230.

hallmarks generally command higher prices than Victorian or later examples. "Flatware", as this class of eating or serving plate is called, can also be bought in a similar variety of patterns in E.P.N.S.—electro-plated nickel silver—introduced by Messrs. Elkingtons of Birmingham in 1840. Although rising, prices for plate are still fairly reasonable even in really good condition. Some firms also used date codes which, combined with the use of Registry Marks by which designs were protected, especially enhances study of the Victorian period. Books on the Victorian decorative arts in general should be constantly consulted as guides to understanding the multiplicity of styles used during that most eclectic but ingenious period.

Silver and plate of the simplified English version of Art Nouveau was made in the 1890s and 1900s by Messrs, Liberty & Co and the Guild of Handicraft with many imitators. It is popular among collectors and consequently expensive, especially when enamelled. Many of the designs used allowed the full natural flowing characteristics of the metal to show themselves, but it should be stressed that misleading modern copies exist of many items, particularly mirror frames and belt-buckles, given away by their modern hallmarks and inept workmanship. The pre-war period was dominated to some extent by the mock-Tudor productions of Omar Ramsden, but selective collecting can be pleasing in this area.

The modern collector should look out for well designed silver and plate (or failing that, chromium-plated or stainless steel wares) made over the last forty to fifty years and should not have to pay too dearly for it. The problem remains that prices are now going to run well into double figures for most good pieces, if not into three at the present rate of inflation. The best advice is to acquire knowledge, especially from handling the objects themselves, with the greatest care and patience before commitment.

Colour plate and Figures 1, 2, 3, 4 and 6 by courtesy of Phillips. Figure 5 by courtesy of Bonhams's.

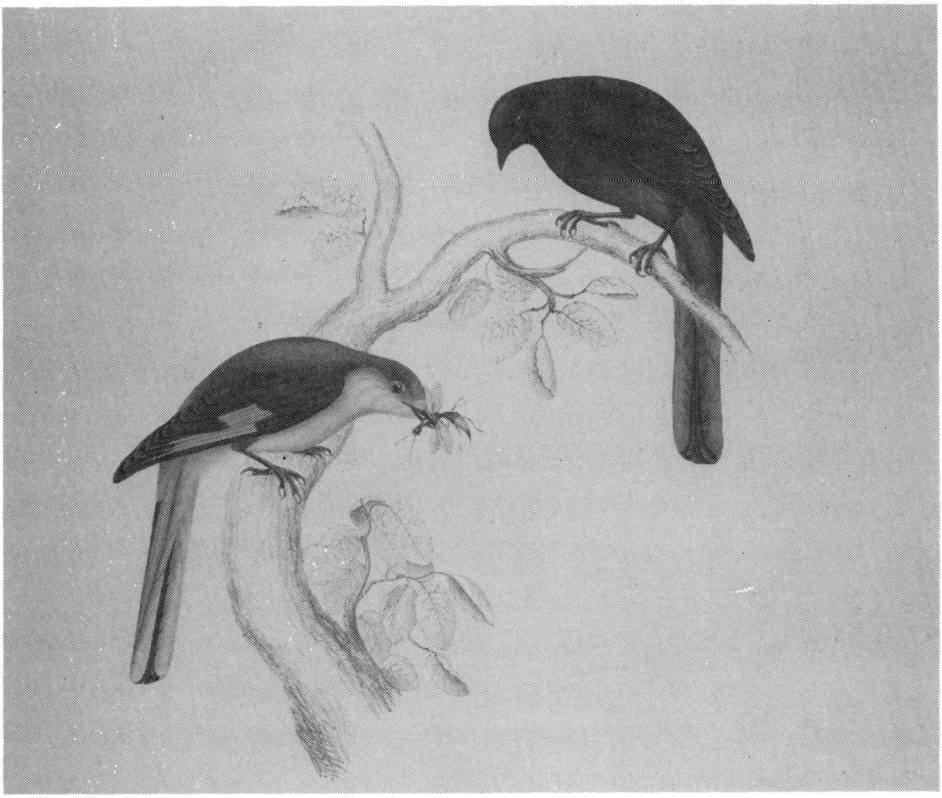

1. A leaf from a French Book of Hours, circa 1460.

CHAPTER FOUR

Books

by Anthony Hobson

A book's a book, although there's nothing in't.

Lord Byron
1788 – 1824

THERE are no trends in book collecting in the sense that there are in women's fashion or interior decoration. Book collectors do not say to themselves on December 31st, 'This year I have been collecting incunabula. What shall it be next year? Beatrix Potter?' Unlike investment buyers or curiosity hunters, they realise, in William Beckford's phrase, that 'There is no obtaining anything worth obtaining without taking the most perseverant pains'; in other words, that it takes diligent search and the determination to outbid competitors for rarities over a span of many years to build up a worth-while collection.

Far from being a prey to fashion the true collector is often sternly (or frivolously) resistant to it. This was already true in the seventeenth century. In his *Advis pour dresser une bibliothèque* (Paris 1628), one of the most influential manuals of advice to collectors, translated into English by John Evelyn, Gabriel Naudé laid down the austere doctrine that books should only be bought for their contents; manuscripts must never be acquired on account of their 'antiquity, illustrations, paintings, binding or other trivial considerations.' Yet there is evidence that contemporary collectors such as Charles-Henri de Clermont, comte de Tonnerre, continued to buy illuminated romances for high prices despite the censure of the intellectual leaders of taste. In much the same way Kipling went on being keenly competed for in the rooms during the period when literary critics were united in despising him, from well before his death in 1936 to long after George Orwell's first rehabilitation in *Horizon* in 1942. This is no doubt because collectors' taste is generally formed in youth and remains constant through changes in fashion.

But though it may be misleading to speak, in the context of this book, of trends in book collecting, there are certainly broader movements of taste which declare themselves over decades rather

2. One of 197 plates from a series of natural history books printed in France between 1801 and 1816.

than single years, fluctuations that the late John Carter in the Sandars Lectures (published by Cambridge University Press in 1948 under the title, *Taste and Technique in Book Collecting),* described as 'distinct rhythms' having 'something of the sweep and regularity of the tides'. The most obvious of these long-term tendencies has been towards a far greater catholicity. Literature of every period now has its supporters; English book-illustration, undervalued in the past, has been promoted by specialised sales in Sotheby's Chancery Lane rooms; while the highly successful sale last year in the same rooms of Mr. J. B. Findlay's library of conjuring books, totalling £81,214, is an illustration of collectors' inventiveness in exploring new fields.

Another tendency has been towards a greater tolerance for blemished copies. Condition has always been, and still is, one of the principal factors affecting price, since the fastidious collector will not accept anything less than a 'fine' copy. (It is interesting to observe that at last the French show signs of adopting what has long been the English and American preference for copies in original condition: unwashed, untampered with and in original or contemporary bindings instead of in heavily gilt morocco by Zaehnsdorf or Lortic.) Association copies continue to command a substantial premium over ones which the author has not given away or inscribed. But below these bibliophilic heights a new market has developed among collectors who have evidently despaired of being able to afford a complete copy, let alone a fine one, of many desirable but expensive books. The prices at Sotheby's sale of the Pottesman incunabula in October 1979 were sometimes astonishing—£528, including the surcharge, for the Rostock *Lactantius* of 1476 lacking more than a hundred leaves—though this figure had been exceeded in June by a single leaf, with illuminated borders but no miniature, from a fourteenth-century Book of Hours on vellum.

Saleroom and booksellers' prices are the first indications of the development of a new 'rhythm', but they are by no means a reliable guide. One of the late Wilmarth S. Lewis's proudest boasts was that during more than fifty years when he was collecting Horace Walpole he succeeded, by a combination of open dealing, wit and charm, with an occasional well-timed show of indignation, in avoiding prices being driven up against himself. There is one class of book for which prices can be seriously misleading, namely those illustrated with colour-plates of flowers, birds, costumes and views. They attract the attention both of the investment buyers, who are more influenced by the movements of the stock market than of artistic taste, and of the 'breakers'—dealers whose trade consists in dismembering such volumes and selling the prints separately. Sotheby's natural history sale in July elicited such high prices—£46,200 for Manetti, Lorenzi and Vanni's *Storia naturale degli uccelli* (Florence

1767-76), more than four times what the previous copy had fetched—that one may surmise that both categories of buyer were active.

When assessing the evidence of auction prices it is important to compare like with like—not a poor copy with a fine one—and to bear in mind that a great sale with an international attendance commands a higher level of price than an ordinary one. As it happens a direct comparison can be made between comparable copies of the same book in Sotheby's sales of two major scientific collections held at a five-year interval: Horblit in November 1974 and Honeyman in November 1979. Both collectors are American, and it is in the United States that the collecting of the historical monuments of science, although practised in England before Queen Victoria's accession, has latterly been most energetically pursued. In the table that follows I have quoted examples of relatively minor books, as well as of major ones, to give a more balanced picture. The Honeyman figures include the 10% surcharge.

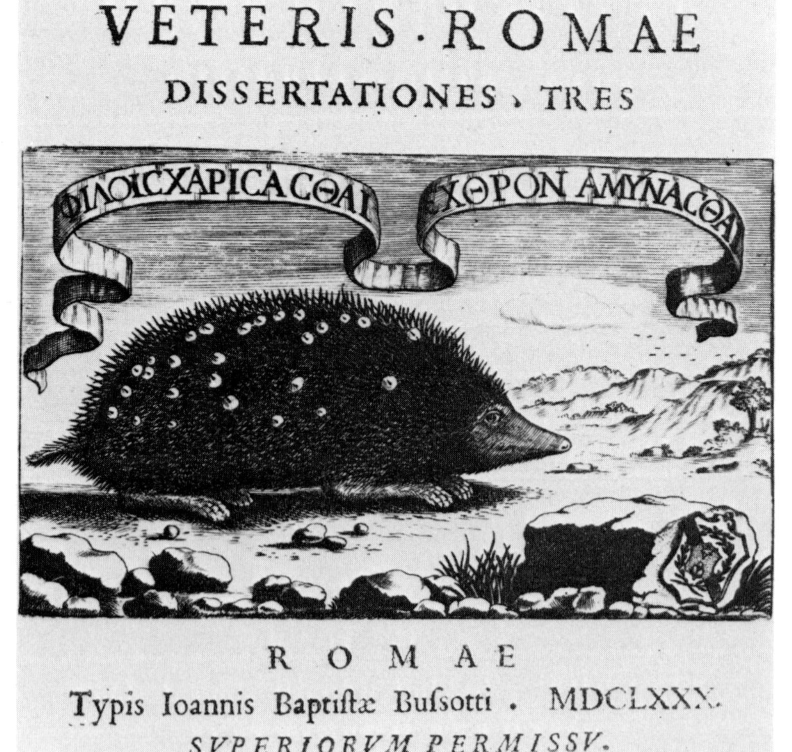

3. From a First edition of *De Aquis et Aquaeductibus,* bound in calf. The book fetched £190 in November 1979.

	Horblit 1974	Honeyman 1979
P. de Fermat. *Varia opera mathematica,* Toulouse 1679, containing researches into the theory of numbers and probability.	£1900	£2200
F. Fontana. *Novae coelestium rerum observationes,* Naples 1646. The first observation of spots on the surface of Mars.	£ 650	£1045
Sigmund Freud. *Die Traumdeutung,* 1900. First edition of 'The interpretation of Dreams'.	£1400	£2970
Galileo Galilei. *Opere,* Bologna 1656. First collected edition.	£ 320	£ 352
T. Garzoni. *Allgemeiner Schauwplatz,* Frankfurt a.M. 1619. First edition in German.	£ 55	£ 99
K. F. Gauss. *Disquisitiones arithmeticae,* Leipzig 1801. First edition of Gauss's proof of the law of quadratic reciprocity.	£ 850	£1430
Gemma Frisius. *De radio astronomico,* Paris 1557.	£ 150	£ 143 (same copy)
Gemma Frisius. *De principiis astronomiae et cosmographiae,* Antwerp 1553.	£ 135	£ 198 (same copy)
Robert H. Goddard. *A method of reaching extreme altitudes,* Washington, D.C., 1919. First edition. A work on the use of rockets to carry instruments to the upper atmosphere by 'the father of modern rocketry'.	£ 550	£ 418
D. Gregory. *Astronomiae . . . elementa,* Geneva 1726.	£ 50	£ 198
James Gregory. *Optica promota,* London 1663. First edition of the first description of the Gregorian reflecting telescope.	£ 800	£1100
Nehemiah Grew. *Musaeum Regalis Societatis,* London 1681.	£ 120	£ 99
N. Grollier de Servière. *Recueil d'ouvrages curieux,* Lyon 1719, with plates of mechanical devices.	£ 240	£ 715
E. Gunter. *The description and use of the Sector,* London 1636. Second edition	£ 160	£ 132
Otto von Guericke. *Experimenta nova,* Amsterdam 1672. First edition, describing the invention of the air-pump and the experiment of the Magdeburg hemispheres.	£1000	£1760 (lacking the portrait)

It is true that the dollar was worth more in relation to the pound in 1974 than in 1979. Nevertheless the general impression is that while works in German or by German authors have moved strongly forward, many other books have hardly kept abreast of inflation, minor works even declining in money terms. Let me add however that the prices paid for the Honeyman copies of the first edition of Galen—£11, 000—and for Harvey's first statement of the circulation of the blood, the notoriously elusive and desirable *De motu cordis* (Frankfurt am Main 1628)—£88,000 (the previous auction record was for a copy sold in Geneva for about £700 in 1948)—made clear that the great monuments of medical

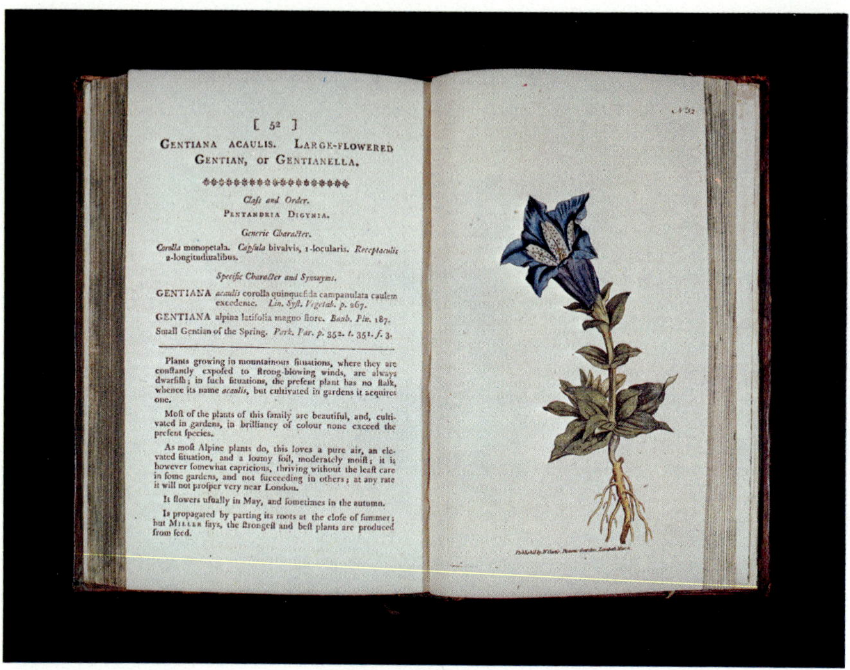

Plate IV. William Curtis. From a 22-volume collection of *The Botanical Magazine* which sold for £4,700 in April 1979.

history are as strongly in demand as ever.

Travel and atlases have been a buoyant market, as the £132,000 (including the surcharge) paid for one of William Hack's manuscript atlases in the Houghton sale at Christie's proved. So have English literary manuscripts; John Fleming gave £82,500 for a notebook containing the earliest draft of Locke's *Essay concerning humane understanding* in the same sale. Prices have moved upwards for fine bindings, the demand for which—since the Henry Davis collection was given to the British Library and the Ehrman collection to the Bodleian—outruns the supply. In a recent bookseller's catalogue £3000 was asked for an Irish eighteenth-century binding, a price nearly six times the highest recorded for an Irish binding in the Abbey sales of 1965-67. Local history and provincial imprints attracted strong support during 1979, noticeably so in Sotheby's September sale in Edinburgh: a tendency that can be paralleled in Italy and in France, where in 1978 the Librairie Paul Jammes issued a pioneering catalogue devoted to *Presses provinciales*.

Finally, what is happening in that notoriously volatile market, modern first editions? Sotheby's decided to separate the sale of modern literary manuscripts and autograph letters, which continue in Bond Street, from modern first editions which are sold in

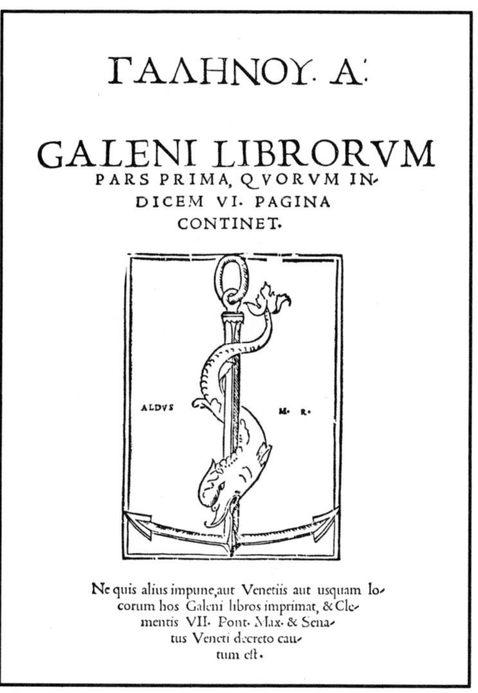
ΓΑΛΗΝΟΥ Α:

GALENI LIBRORVM
PARS PRIMA, QVORVM IN-
DICEM VI· PAGINA
CONTINET·

ALDVS M· R·

Ne quis alius impune, aut Venetiis aut usquam lo-
corum hos Galeni libros imprimat, & Cle-
mentis VII· Pont· Max· & Sena-
tus Veneti decreto cau-
tum est·

4. Galen, first edition in Greek, 1525. In November 1979 it sold for £11,000.

NICOLAI JOSEPHI JACQUIN
SELECTARUM STIRPIUM
AMERICANARUM
HISTORIA,
IN QUA
AD LINNÆANUM SYSTEMA
DETERMINATÆ DESCRIPTÆQUE SIS-
-TUNTUR PLANTÆ ILLÆ, QUAS IN
INSULIS MARTINICA, JAMAICA, DO-
-MINGO, ALIISQUE, ET IN VICINÆ
CONTINENTIS PARTE, OBSERVA-
-VIT RARIORES; ADJECTIS ICONI-
-BUS AD AUTORIS ARCHE-
-TYPA PICTIS.

5. Watercolour and gouache title page, circa 1781.

Chancery Lane. The most spectacular recent sale of moderns, that of Jonathan Goodwin's collection, took place in New York in 1977. The Goodwin prices and those paid at one of Chancery Lane's regular bi-annual sales in July 1979 make an interesting comparison.

	Goodwin 1977	*Chancery Lane 1979*
James Joyce. *Ulysses,* 1936. First English edition, specially bound and signed.	$2250	£ 693
D. H. Lawrence. *Lady Chatterley's Lover,* 1928. First edition. One of 1000 copies, signed.	$ 650	£ 126.50
D. H. Lawrence. *Sun,* 1928. Presentation copy	$1100	£ 407
G. Bernard Shaw. *Saint Joan,* 1924. First edition, inscribed.	$ 425	£ 115.50

I do not think these results indicate any real falling off in the interest in Joyce, Lawrence and Shaw—though the last-named is probably overdue for a decline. Rather they prove the difference in price to be expected at a great sale and at an ordinary one.

Both sales provided other indications that deserve noting. The Goodwin copy of Nancy Cunard's anthology *Negro,* of 1934, a book that ten years ago was steady at £40, sold for $1500: a reflection of the desperate search by American university librarians

6. Description of the Battle of Marengo by Louis Alexandre Berthier and bound for Napoleon. It fetched £3,200 in May 1979.

for source-books to be used in black study courses. First World War authors did well at Chancery Lane—presentation copies of Siegfried Sassoon's first book (*Poems,* 1906) made £946 and of his *Orpheus in Diloeryum,* 1908, £572, and Henry Williamson's *The Star-Born* 1933, one of seventy copies, made £176 (a price that seems to have taken the auctioneers by surprise)—and T. E. Lawrence retains his popularity. But Sir Winston Churchill, it is sad to see, was in full retreat: *The Story of the Malakand Field Force,* 1898, £126.50 (£170.50 in 1977), *London to Ladysmith via Pretoria,*

1900, £11 (from £30.80 to £44 in 1978), *Lord Randolph Churchill,* 1906, £11 (£27.50 in 1978).

A curiosity of the post-War book world has been the emergence of new 'collected' authors as a result of their treatment in a biographical work of exceptional brilliance. The late A. N. L. Munby's witty and humane *Phillipps Studies* transformed the irascible baronet into a cult object—centenary exhibitions were held in London and New York, and H. P. Kraus issued a catalogue devoted entirely to Phillippica—and Carter and Pollard's *An enquiry into the nature of certain nineteenth-century pamphlets* performed the same service for T. J. Wise. (John Carter's copy of Wise's best known forgery, Elizabeth Barrett Browning's 'Reading' *Sonnets,* sold for £1800 in 1976, more than it would have fetched if genuine.) A. J. A. Symonds's *Quest for Corvo* effected a similar apotheosis for Frederick Rolfe, and it is noteworthy that the only lot to fetch a higher price at Chancery Lane in July than in the Goodwin sale was Rolfe's first book (one that neatly combines his two predominant interests), *Tarcissus, the boy martyr of Rome* (Saffron Walden, c. 1880): Goodwin $1700, Chancery Lane £990.

When studying the results of 'modern' sales one has the sensation of looking into a wild life reserve. Young animals thrust vigorously forward, noble beasts courageously defend their territory, while others weaken and are trampled underfoot. Here is a field where the play of collectors' preferences can be observed in its pure form, unadulterated by the competition of investors or breakers.

Colour plate and Figures 1 and 6 by courtesy of Phillips. Figures 2, 3, 4 and 5 by courtesy of Sotheby's.

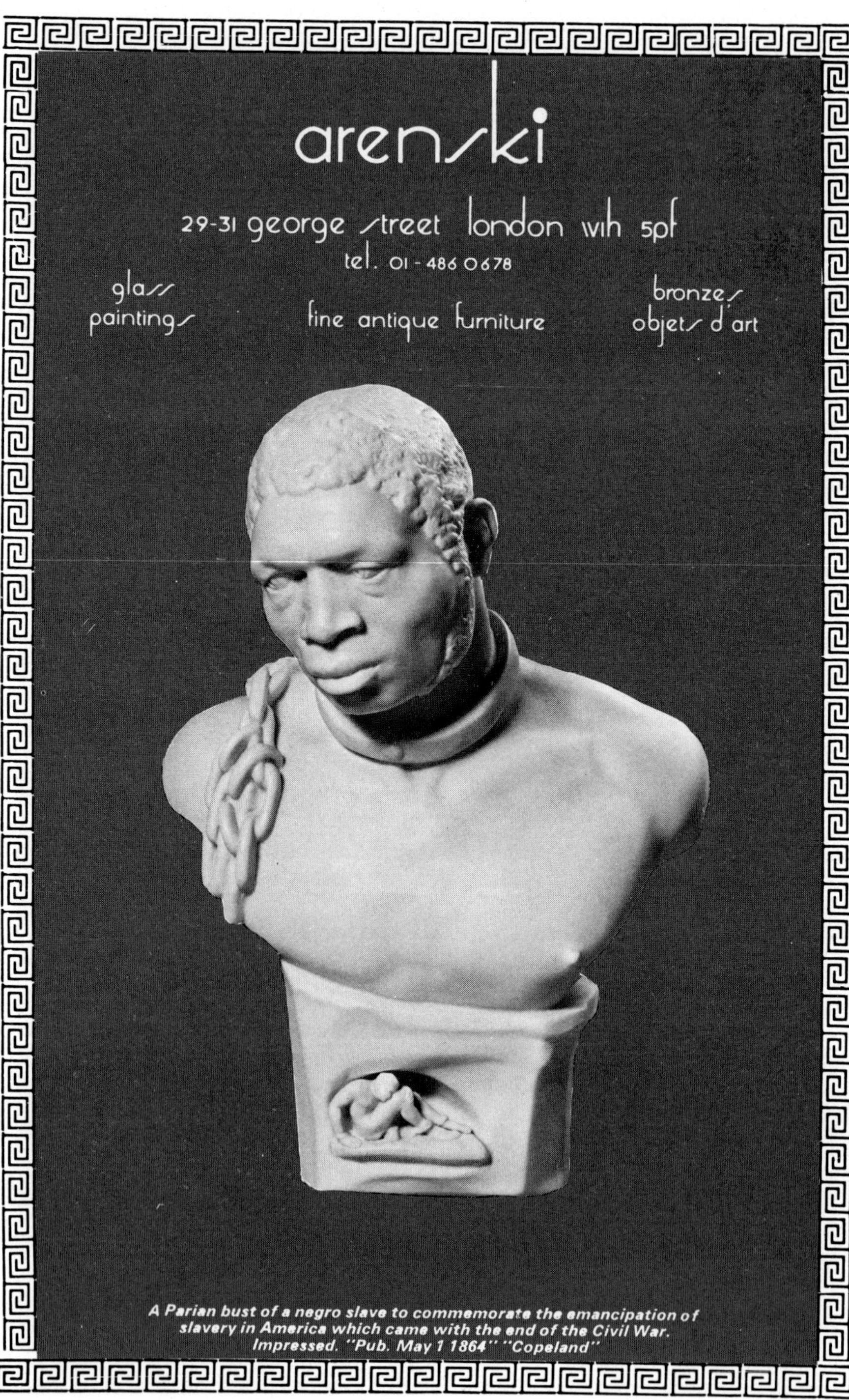
arenski
29-31 george street london w1h 5pf
tel. 01-486 0678
glass
paintings
fine antique furniture
bronzes
objets d'art

Plate V. 'An absolute dazzle of scarlet and gold' this lacquer bureau-bookcase fetched £38,000 at Christie's.

CHAPTER FIVE
Furniture
by Patrick Macnaghten

As our delight or as our treasure;
The whole is either our cupboard of food
Or cabinet of pleasure.

George Herbert
1593 – 1633

THE person who buys an old stamp almost certainly does so because he is a stamp collector. But the person who buys an antique chair probably simply wants something nice to sit on. Nor is the person necessarily a man. While collecting stamps or coins appeals practically exclusively to men choosing anything for the home is virtually a woman's prerogative. The consequence is that furniture, appealing as it does to so many people for so many reasons, has a wide range of fashion simultaneously.

The classic pieces of the 18th century never really go out of fashion. Prices have of course risen inexorably with inflation, like a moored boat rising gently on an incoming tide, and have just about doubled over the past five years. This does not mean, however, that such pieces are any more in fashion now than they were then, nor any less. What has happened is that they have been joined in popular favour by two other types of period furniture. One is the Victorian, the other oak and allied woods such as yew, beech and elm both early and late. An indication of the meteoric rise in Victoriana is illustrated by the set of pretty seat furniture shown at Fig. 6. Comprising a 'gentleman's chair' (with arms), a 'lady's chair' (without arms to allow for the spread of the crinoline) and three side chairs (only one shown in the photograph), this set fetched £200 in Bonham's auction rooms in May 1975. That was considered a fair price at the time but today the same set would be unlikely to fetch less than £1,000.

Fairly recently Phillips obtained £400 and £340 respectively for two Charles I oak joint stools which ten years previously would probably have fetched under £20. A similar but much more elaborate stool fetched as much as £1,350 in the same auction rooms. At the other end of the time scale prices for this category of furniture are also high. The Windsor chair—the name comes from the Buckinghamshire beechwoods where these chairs were

1. Beautiful yet practical. A walnut bureau-bookcase of the time of George I.

2. At the end of 1979 this early 17th century oak table fetched £2,300.

and are made—illustrated at Fig. 5 happens to have been made of yew and this would add a little to its value. It fetched £540 at Bonham's in January 1979. Its stretcher of H-formation and its general sturdiness suggest a date of about 1830. Both material and date are less important in explaining the comparatively high value of this piece than the images it conjures up of a farmhouse kitchen where 'the bacon's on the rafter, the wine is in the wood, and God who made good laughter has seen that they are good.'*

But if the rising tide of inflation has buoyed up the prices of the most fashionable types of furniture it has sunk less sea-worthy craft. Junk is out. In times of affluence a new lower limit intrudes itself into the antiques market. People who find that they can now just afford antiques start buying them and people who cannot quite afford the lowliest antiques buy the next best thing—elderly secondhand stuff. Then, as soon as stringency replaces prosperity this bottom end of the market disappears. 1979 was one of the years which saw this happen. Nobody wants the flimsy or shoddy mass production of the 20th century in spite of the fact that the pieces of the same period which are good in workmanship and design are assured of finding a good home.

But a discerning public now insists that furniture, however attractive, must work for its living. It is only with those types of pieces which soar through the sound barrier to reach the rarified atmosphere inhabited by very rich collectors that practicality is of no account. One of the classic, sought-after pieces of antique furniture is that eminently practical kind of dining-table with its top supported by two or three central pillars so that the wooden

* *The wicked Grocer.* By G. K. Chesterton

3. Dutch marqueterie of all periods has been selling strongly for some years. This fine centre table, *c.* 1810, would fetch £1,500-£2,000.

legs are well out of the way of the human ones. Such a table at which the diners can converse easily with those opposite to them is worth about three times as much as a table of similar type and quality which is so wide that they have to shout across a gleaming expanse of mahogany.

It is only collectors who do not worry about such things. For instance, the gorgeous lacquer bureau-bookcase shown in colour, an absolute dazzle of scarlet and gold, fetched £38,000 at Christie's. One could, however, keep just as many books in, and write just as many letters comfortably at, the George I walnut bureau-bookcase (Fig. 1) which Bonham's sold for £2,500 in December 1978. The delicate charm of the walnut with its soft warm colouring and beautifully figured grain is in an entirely different category from the flamboyant glory of the vivid lacquer. Each is at the top of its class but the classes are in different schools.

The use of walnut for furniture came into fashion with the Restoration of Charles II in 1660, stayed for sixty or seventy years, declined for about a hundred and swung back about 1830 to remain in favour throughout Victorian times. Walnut antiques are in fashion today, rather surprisingly perhaps, considering how vulnerable this wood is to the effects of central heating. Except for chairs, it is usually found as veneer which is cut across the grain of the tree like slices of a Swiss roll. These veneers are mounted on hardwood carcases made from timber cut lengthways along the

4. A set of eight mahogany dining chairs of George III period which fetched £7,000 in September 1978 included this elbow chair.

trunk. The consequence is that when the two woods dry out—a process greatly accelerated by the atmosphere generated by central heating—one shrinks one way and the other at rightangles to it so that the veneer splits and curls. But in spite of its faults walnut remains popular. It fits in well with almost any scheme of decoration because it suffuses the whole room with a cosy glow, and its delicate grain makes it as good to look at close to as its architectural proportions do from a distance.

The 'Walnut Period' ended abruptly in the 1720s. The majority

5. Sturdy country furniture is becoming very fashionable. This Windsor chair c. 1830 fetched £540 in January 1979.

of the timber came to England from the area round Grenoble and a particularly severe winter in the first decade of the 18th century had the same disastrous effect on the trees as Dutch elm disease has had in our own times. The French banned the export of walnut in 1720 and the cabinetmakers of England had to look elsewhere. There were two alternative sources of supply, the Mediterranean coast and Virginia, but neither found much favour with English

6. The type of Victorian furniture which has become increasingly popular in the past five years.

cabinetmakers. Mediterranean wood lacked the lively grain of the Grenoble variety and the Virginian was a dark rather dull wood with a purplish tinge. In any case it was expensive and for the same cost they could, and did, obtain mahogany from the West Indies.

Mahogany proved to be a wonderful wood, ideal for carving as well as for veneers. It has been to cabinetmakers what silver is to the makers of jewellery ever since. For the last two decades of the 18th century and the first three of the 19th many exotic woods were introduced but none completely ousted mahogany. Satinwood, with its smooth golden sheen, was well suited to the elegant purity of the neo-classical styles, as was the dark strongly marked grain of rosewood to the exuberance of the Regency. The Victorians dutifully followed Prince Albert's lead in furnishing their houses with maplewood but soon reverted to walnut, a much prettier wood than the brash yellow maple. Later in the century they moved away from lightness and prettiness and went in for heavy oak stained sticky black and mahogany with brick dust rubbed into it until it took the colour of oxblood. But today it is the daintier pieces of Victoriana which command the high prices.

While prices obviously have their effect on fashion and vice versa, factors other than fashion have their effect too. Quite a short time ago English antiques, regardless of period or style, were apt to take a one-way trip across the Atlantic but this is no longer the case. The reason is not a change in fashion in America but simply a change in economics. The growing strength of the pound has made England an expensive place for American tourists and dealers to shop, and they are turning their attention more and more towards their own fine Colonial furniture which is freer and less formal than the English styles from which it derived.

The Dutch, too, have ceased to regard England as a happy hunting ground for bargains. However, they are still buying back antiques which originated in their own country, and this has kept up the prices of good marqueterie. The fine example of Dutch craftsmanship shown in Fig. 3 would probably fetch between £1,500 and £2,000 today, about twice as much as would an English table of similar design and date but without the inlay.

It is not altogether chauvinistic to claim that English marqueterie is better than Dutch for, seen side by side, the English has more depth of detail. If you came across a leaf or flower petal from Dutch marqueterie it would look like a strangely-shaped piece of holly or sycamore, whereas a similar chip detached from English marqueterie would still be quite obviously a leaf or petal. Probably the best collection of marqueterie in the world can be seen at the Rijksmuseum in Amsterdam and pride of place there is given to a really superb looking glass with a marqueterie frame made in England.

German furniture is not, and never has been, very fashionable in England, being generally considered to be coarse and florid. Nevertheless the Deutschmark is strong enough for German dealers to compete with each other for any pieces which appear on the English market. The number of books recently published throw new light on the history of German furniture and direct interest towards it.

The pound is now drawing away from the lira but Italian furniture, although not as eagerly sought by Italians as it was until quite recently, remains in favour in England, particularly Renaissance oak and walnut.

French furniture has always been regarded as the most 'collectable' of all and has the immense advantage, from a collector's point of view, that the cabinetmakers were obliged by law to sign their products. For example, Phillips sold a Bureau Plat of the Louis XV period signed by I. Dubois, for £13,500. Admittedly it was a fine piece, elegant as these writing tables always are, its serpentine top inset with a panel of gilt tooled leather and edged with ormolu. All the same, without the stamp of the maker's name it would have been unlikely to reach such a high price. A much less desirable piece, though very good of its type, was the provincial chest of drawers of the same period which reached a bid of £3,000.

One significant feature of 1979 was that for the first time English furniture of the first quality began to rival French under the auctioneer's hammer. Among the reasons for this could well be the fresh information which is even now coming to light about

18th century cabinet makers, as epitomised by Christopher Gilbert's splendid work on Thomas Chippendale. In November 1979 Christie's sold a commode with a highly probable attribution to Langlois, who worked in England in the latter half of the 18th century for £22,000. That the estimate was £5000/7000 is not so much evidence of pessimism on the auctioneer's part as enthusiasm on that of the people attending the sale. A satin wood commode in the same sale fetched £7,500 against the estimate of £3,000/4,000 but a nice little Davenport of the late Regency went for £600 instead of the expected £700/900—a salutary reminder that, below the realms of the collector, the public is turning away from furniture, however attractive, if it is not useful and usable. Even Victorian Davenports have not risen in price to anything like the same extent as their contemporary pieces which are more practical.

It is this selectivity which, more than anything else, set the fashion in antique furniture in 1979.

Colour plate by courtesy of Christie's. Figures 1, 3, 5 and 6 by courtesy of Bonham's. Figure 2 by courtesy of Sotheby's. Figure 4 by courtesy of Phillips.

1. Spring Table Clock by Edward Burgis, London, circa 1685.

CHAPTER SIX
Clocks
by Michael G. Cox

'Pray, my dear,' quoth my mother, 'have you not forgot to wind up the clock?'

Laurence Sterne
1713–1768

IN THE last ten years the interest in clocks has grown to an unprecedented degree,to the point that today there is hardly anything in the clock field which is not desired by somebody and therefore has a value at which it will change hands.

In this article I will have to confine myself, for reasons of space, to certain categories of English clocks with the one exception of French Carriage Clocks. However, before discussing these, I feel it is neccessary to go into a little historical background.

The golden era of English clockmaking is considered to be that between 1660 and 1750. This is, generally speaking, true though it must be said that many fine clocks were made in England in the balance of the 18th century, throughout the 19th and in the very early years of the 20th century. The Worshipful Company of Clockmakers was founded in 1631 when Charles I granted the Company its charter and the split of the clockmakers and the blacksmiths finally took place. With the restoration of the monarchy in 1660, English clockmaking flowered thanks to the inventiveness and skill of such men as Edward East, Ahasuerus Fromanteel, William Clement, Henry Jones, Thomas Tompion, Joseph Knibb, his brothers John and Samuel, Daniel Quare just to name a few.

Perhaps the single most important horological development of the 17th century was the discovery of the pendulum by Christiaan Huygens of Holland, and its practical application to clocks made possible through Huygens' co-operation with Saloman Coster, the eminent Dutch clockmaker. Credit for the introduction of this device to the United Kingdom must go to the Fromanteel family. The Commonwealth Mercury of November 1658 carried their advertisement which in part reads: "There is lately a way found for making clocks that go exact and keep equaller time than any now made without this regulator . . . and may be made to go a week or

2. Lantern clock by John Knibb, Oxford, circa 1685.

a month or a year, with one winding up . . . and is very excellent for all house clocks that go either with springs or weights. . . Made by Ahasuerus Fromanteel, who made the first that were in England". The invention of the pendulum was the keystone to the production of fine 17th century clocks, because it enabled the cabinetmaker to produce a thin and elegant case and the clockmaker to introduce accurate timekeeping.

The Clockmakers' Company held sway over the London clockmakers, but did not have power outside the city of London. The Company's rules were rigidly enforced and the standards of London clockmaking were uniformly high, which is perhaps why London-made clocks were most desirable in their day, and are equally prized now, at the end of the 20th century. It is worth while noting here that both longcase clocks and spring table clocks of the late 17th century were expensive when they were first made and are expensive to buy today.

As time progressed and the 17th century gave way to the 18th clockmaking had become a more widely practised art and many more clockmakers were working than had been doing so fifty years earlier. It is safe to say that by 1750 the high standards which had already been set were now inherent in the trade. Thus it was that the Clockmakers' Company powers ceased to have so much force after 1750 and most probably the need for such force had long vanished because of the clockmakers' natural pride in their workmanship.

So perhaps at this point, I can move on to discuss individual types of clock. I have tried to select categories which may be more frequently and easily found, rather than the clocks of great rarity or complication, of which perhaps only one or two examples were ever made, and anyway can only be seen in museums or private collections.

Lantern Clocks

The term lantern clock correctly defined in its simplest form is a clock with a posted-frame movement, which means that behind its dial is an arrangement of wheels and pinions held in their correct position by means of posts, i.e. flat strips of brass with holes in them to accommodate the pivots of the wheels and the pinions. Sometimes these clocks are called Cromwellian clocks, Sheep's Head or Ram's Head clocks, but for the sake of clarity the name lantern clock is probably most widely used and is the best choice. These were the first domestic clocks, and in pretty much the same form appeared from the time of Elizabeth I's reign in the 16th century to the end of the first quarter of the 18th century, though they continued to be made by English country clockmakers until the end of the 18th century—a span of some 225 years.

Some were signed by the maker and some were not, but the fact that they were not signed does not necessarily detract from their value today. To my mind, the single most important factor when buying these clocks is their originality. Unfortunately lantern clocks, perhaps by the very nature of their construction, which is simple and fairly crude, have been open to the poorest of repairs, and indeed whole clocks have been built from scratch in recent years, subjected to aging processes and offered as genuine 17th/18th century clocks. Of course, this is faking.

However, a good example with the maker's name engraved upon it can be found in the sale room for around £1,000 and as much as several thousands depending upon its general condition, the maker and, of course, the originality.

I think it might be well to digress for a moment and say that, in common with so many works of art and antiques, buying clocks of any kind is something that should be done through a competent dealer. The pitfalls are numerous. In the first place, you have to consider the visual exterior, be it in a combination of wood and brass, or simply brass on its own. Secondly, you must consider the movement, or mechanical side of the clock. Although there are numerous books on the subject of clocks, both general and specialist in their nature there is no substitute for long experience in actually handling clocks. The specialist dealer knows his business, and although you will pay more for the clock in his showroom, you will be able to buy with confidence, because he has done all the 'vetting' for you. The clock will be what it is supposed to be and also will be in proper mechanical order to continue performing its function for many years.

Longcase Clocks

These clocks are probably the ones with the most universal appeal and have been in homes from the most humble cottage to the grand manor house since the 17th century. Commonly referred to as "Grandfather Clocks", the origin of this name is obscure, but generally is attributed to a song called "The Grandfather's Clock" composed by an American, named Henry Clay Work, and published after the American Civil War (1861-1865). It sold 800,000 copies and brought the Composer $4,000,00 in royalties. There are other theories including a statement in "A Short Dictionary of Furniture", London 1952, by John Gloag stating that the term was first used in 1878.

Longcase clock is the term I shall use. Fine examples of these by the best London makers appear in a variety of cases and dial sizes. From 1660 onwards cases were commonly walnut veneered on oak, with the walnut being either a well marked burr, or plain. Occasionally the cabinetmaker chose more exotic veneers such as olive-wood oysters, laburnum oysters, mulberry and sometimes ebony. Dial sizes vary from 10″ square (sometimes marginally smaller) in the 1670s through 11″ square in the late 1680s and 1690s to 12″ square in the early 1700s. The use of parquetry (geometric

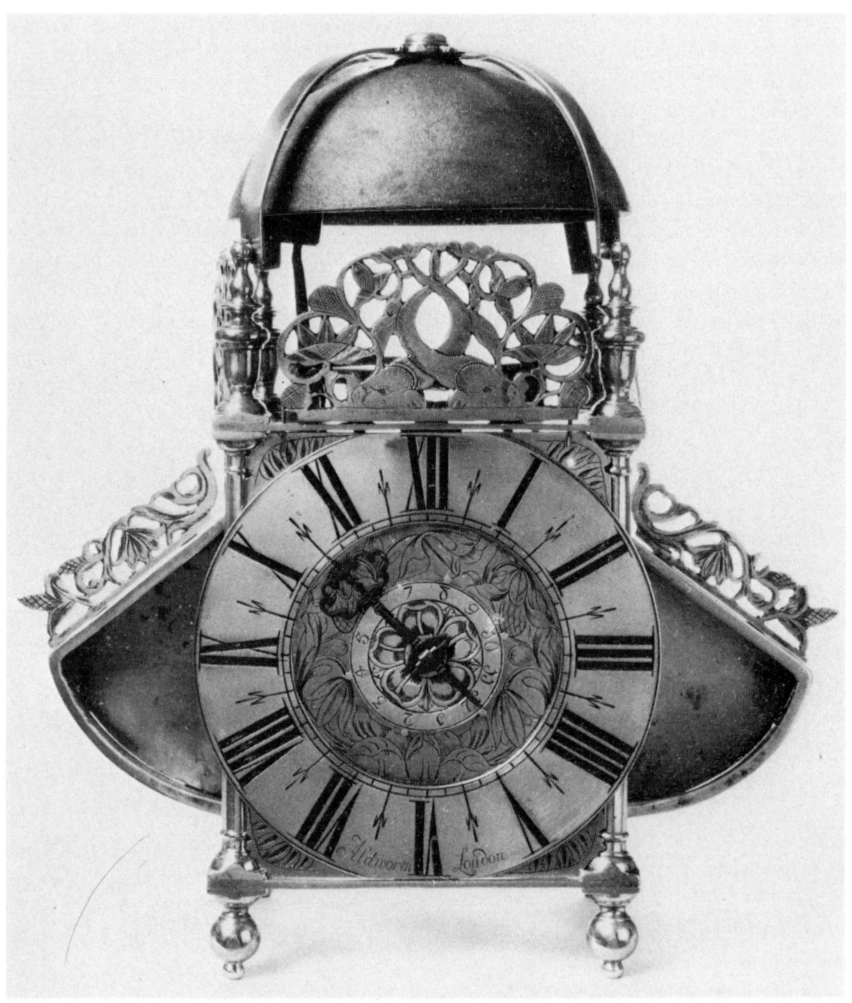

3. 'Batwing' lantern clock by Samuel Aldworth, London, circa 1690.

inlay) decoration usually occurs on the early longcases of the 1670s which led to the various forms of marquetry consisting of inlaid panels illustrating birds and flowers and culminating in the all-over marquetry known as 'seaweed' or 'arabesque'.

The square brass dials, consisting of silvered chapter rings, seconds rings (where fitted), blued steel hands, brass spandrels and sometimes calendar apertures, are attached to weight-driven and hour striking movements of varying duration, but most commonly of eight days, in the case of London clocks. Far less common is the month going clock and very rare are those which go for three months, or a year.

By contrast with the London clockmakers, the country

longcases of the early 18th century were made of solid oak, or other hard and soft woods, also the 30-hour movement was commonly used, which was an adaptation of the Lantern clock posted frame movement.

The square dial disappeared from London clocks by 1720 to be replaced by the arch dial, though the square dial continued in use by country makers for another fifty years. Movements in the 18th century became more elaborate and some were fitted with quarter striking, or musical work, as well as subsidiary dials for lunar work, or tidal indications and even automata work in the arch of the dials. By the mid 18th century, mahogany was a popular and widely used veneer for clock cases of all kinds and practically eliminated the use of walnut and other veneers. Mahogany enjoyed enormous popularity in the second half of the 18th century and throughout the 19th century.

Prices of longcase clocks vary enormously and for a wide variety of reasons, such as date, maker, originality and function. Those shown in the table below are just a very rough guide of prices you might have been expected to pay in 1979 in the sale rooms. However, all clocks which have been bought in the sale room will certainly need cleaning and restoration. It must be borne in mind that this is an added cost. Finally, and I cannot stress this matter too highly, these prices are for clocks, which, although dirty and in need of attention, are basically precisely what they are supposed to be and certainly are not for "marriage" i.e. wrong movements with wrong cases, etc.

17th century	
10″ square dial, walnut, London made, 8-day movement	£4,000–£16,000
10″ square dial, marquetry, London made, 8–day movement	£6,000–£20,000
12″ square dial, walnut, London made, 8–day movement	£2,500–£4,000
18th century	
10″ square dial, oak, country made, 30-hour movement	£250–£500
10″ square dial, oak, country made, 8-day movement	£400–£700
Arch dial, mahogany, London made, 8-day movement	£1,000–£2,000

Bracket Clocks

More correctly these clocks should be called Spring Table Clocks, because the decoration of the backplates of their movements with beautiful engraving was assuredly put there for people to see, which they could not do, if the clocks were sitting on wall brackets. Clocks were expensive in the 17th century, and even the wealthy probably owned only one or possibly two. I believe they were taken upstairs at night and set on brackets in hallways where they could be heard striking by anyone who was wakeful. Thus, because they were moved from a piece of furniture downstairs to a bracket upstairs, they were more generally known by the name

Plate VI. Longcase clock by Edward Burgis, London circa 1675.

4. Longcase clock by Thomas Tompion, London, circa 1700.

5. Bracket clock by Daniel Delander, London, circa 1725.

of their secondary position.

The choice of woods for the case of these clocks basically followed the same pattern as the longcase clocks, though marquetry work was seldom used. A good 17th or 18th century bracket is a pleasing piece to own and versatile from the point of view that it will fit into any room of the house and complement a piece of furniture.

Until well into the 18th century, Bracket Clocks were generally speaking the product of the London Clockmaker. Fine examples by Thomas Tompion fetch £12,000 upwards in the sale rooms and this year. Christie's sold a famous one, known as the 'Sussex Tompion' for £65,000. This particular clock dates to circa 1676–1680, and may possibly be the earliest Tompion repeating clock; the 8–day movement is fitted with grande-sonnerie striking. The purpose of fitting repeating work was to enable a person to determine the time at night, therefore clocks so equipped could be kept by the bedside. Grande sonnerie striking tells the last hour and the number of quarters past it and is the most complex of the various forms of striking.

Like Longcases, Bracket Clocks had square dials in the 17th century and arched dials from about 1705–1708 onwards. Their movements were almost invariably from the very beginning (c. 1680) of 8–days duration and initially employed a "verge" escapement with short bob pendulum, which continued in use almost to the end of the 18th century; in the 18th century the "anchor" escapement came into use, because it was considered a more accurate time-keeping device. Our Victorian ancestors in the belief that everything prior to their era was mere prologue, converted many "verge" bracket clocks to "anchor" escapement for good time-keeping. Clocks, which have been so converted, are worth considerably less than those which are original "verge".

Prices again vary from a low of say, £1,200 to a high of, say, £15,000. The same remarks which I made in connection with longcase clock prices apply. A good 17th century bracket clock by a London maker (not one of the great names) will sell for £4,000–£6,000. A good 18th century example will range from £1,500–£2500. If the clock has musical work, quarter-striking and/or other complications, then it will be more expensive.

French Carriage Clocks

Such has been the price rise in these clocks in the past ten years that whereas in the 1950s and 1960s they were popular wedding gifts, this is not true in the 1970s unless the donor is feeling very generous. People who bought them in the 1950s for £20 were fortunate.

The French Carriage Clock industry reached its height of production in the latter part of the 19th century.

In its simplest form, it is a timepiece (non-striking clock) in a

6. Bracket clock by William Hughes, London, circa 1770.

glass and brass case standing about 5½″ high. In its most complex form, it can be grande sonnerie striking, repeating at will, with subsidiary dials for perpetual calendar and lunar work, with Sèvres porcelain panels to the dial, sides and back door, all contained in a mercurially fire-gilt engraved case. The price can run from £100, or less, to several thousands of pounds.

England was France's best customer for these clocks and literally thousands of them were imported and sold here. Prices varied according to the quality of the case and its movement and so, literally there was something to suit every pocket. Fine though this was, when the clocks were new, it is a very different matter today when those which were made *down* to a price come up for sale, because the chances are that the movements are substantially worn out and will cost a great deal more to put right than they cost to buy. Generally, the French put their best movements into 'gorge' cases and some of these movements were marked with the maker's monogram, or trade-mark, and a very few by the best makers were fully signed on the backplate (a further indication of quality). Clocks, so cased and marked, are the most desirable and command higher figures in the sale room.

All illustrations by courtesy of Michael G. Cox.

J. & M. BRISTOW

Antiques

28 LONG STREET, TETBURY, GLOS.

Tel.: Tetbury 52222

THE COUNTRY CLOCK SPECIALISTS

Antique Clocks & Barometers bought & sold, also stocked choice pieces of furniture from 17th. & 18th. centuries.

To maintain our stock we wish to purchase all types of Antique Clocks and Barometers, any condition considered.

George White

FORMERLY WHITE, BONIFACE

8 High Street, Thornbury, Bristol BS12 2AQ
Tel: Thornbury (0454) 413172

Our stock consists of a small select collection of 17th and 18th century LONGCASE, LANTERN and BRACKET CLOCKS, all carefully restored on the premises, situated not more than a few minutes drive from the intersection of the M4 & M5 motorways.

1. A large Victorian tavern measure, pewter.

CHAPTER SEVEN
A Saturday Morning Stroll
by Magpie

Tis sweet to him who all the week
Through city crowds must push his way,
To stroll alone . . .

Samuel Taylor Coleridge
1772 – 1834

THERE is a deliciously guilty feeling about browsing round antiques shops and market stalls. It is such a glorious waste of time which, one knows, really ought to be devoted to some worthwhile task like mowing the lawn or doing the household accounts. But to enjoy the full savour of these stolen moments it is necessary to have some permanent reminder of them. To return empty-handed would be quite indefensible. Something must be bought, even if it is something for which one has very little use. In fact, that is part of the fun. There are few more satisfying luxuries than buying something you don't need with money you can't afford.

To get the best out of Saturday morning dawdling one should have an open mind, ready to consider anything which is offered. The serious search for an item to add to a collection requires a quite different approach. Saturday strollers are out to enjoy themselves, purpose enough in itself. They are acquirers rather than collectors.

Boxes have an enormous attraction for the acquirer. Snuff boxes, patch boxes, pill boxes—anything from a gold and enamel example of 18th century art and taste to a fifty-year-old tin for toffees. The purchase of boxes, particularly the humbler sort, can always be justified. ("So useful for keeping stamps in"). But perhaps usefulness, however far-fetched, is not really a qualification for something to be bought on impulse from a market stall. Usefulness smacks of a rational approach, the last thing the Saturday stroller wants. He must be free as air to be as utterly irresponsible as his heart desires. If he sees something looking like an archaic bicycle wheel in the dim corner of a shop he must be prepared to investigate, to inspect, to bargain, to buy, and finally to bear home in triumph. It may of course be all that remains of a penny-farthing cycle, or it may be a waywiser.

'Waywiser' was the colloquial name for a perambulator, a

2. 'Waywiser', 'Hodometer', and 'Perambulator' are alternative names for this distance-measuring instrument.

scientific instrument used in the 18th and 19th centuries for measuring distance. It consists of a large wooden wheel, shod with an iron tyre and held in a fork like the front wheel of a bicycle. Above the fork is a dial usually showing yards, poles, furlongs and miles, and finally some sort of handle. Depending upon the market for which it was made, the waywiser can be a crude work-a-day affair or an elaborate piece of craftsmanship with a delicately chased dial and a mahogany handle gracefully shaped to accommodate a dilettante's lilywhite hands. But whoever they were made for all waywisers have one thing in common and that is that they are extremely accurate.

The Army was much hampered in its attempts to defeat the Jacobite invasion of 1745 by the inadequacy of existing maps, and as a consequence a complete survey of England was ordered. It was begun in 1782 and so accurate were the waywisers that a later check disclosed that by the time the survey was complete it was only less than a quarter of a mile out. Most big estates had their waywisers and even agents who were unversed in trigonometry could push them round the edges of fields and so assess the acreage for rental purposes.

When in Regency times, John Macadam invented his system of paving roads with flints chipped into six-ounce weights waywisers came into fashion as amusing ways of enjoying a walk. They glided along quite easily on the metalled surfaces so no great strength was needed to push them. That determined young lady Dorothy Wordsworth badgered the agent at Racedown, the house in Dorset which the Pinney family had lent to her and her brother, to retrieve the waywiser from their other estate so that she could measure the distance to Crewkerne. Trundling it up and down the steep hills on the Dorset-Somerset border must have been good preparation for her later life among the mountains of the Lake District.

So familiar a sight was the waywiser on the highways and byways that when the first high-wheeled baby carriages appeared they were mockingly dubbed perambulators and the good old measuring instrument gradually lost its official name.

Some Saturday strollers are less dedicated to the principle of buying extravagantly than others, and there may be those who will cavil at paying a lot of money for something as completely useless as a waywiser, for a really good one, made by a renowned instrument maker, can fetch as much as £500 or £600. For them, too, there is a wide and fascinating choice. An engraved glass Victorian fingerbowl, for instance, the last survivor of a set, or perhaps a pewter plate, battered and far from flat. Pewter was the third stage in dining table furnishing. First came the hunk or slice of bread on which the meat was placed, known by the Norman-French word *tranche* anglicised to trench, then trencher, and it continued to be applied to the second stage, the wooden plate.

3. A gold-mounted tortoiseshell snuffbox, French, circa 1750.

Wooden plates must have been less messy than bread and it is unlikely that anybody bothered much about washing them up. Pewter plates are singularly difficult to wash unless the water is very hot—which it probably seldom was in centuries gone by—but they have the inestimable advantage of being almost impossible to break. Pewter is an alloy of lead and tin and will take quite a high polish if needed as an ornament. However, when it is dull it looks very much like the whiter Britannia metal, a cheaper substitute. A good rule of thumb for the inexperienced is that pewter feels heavier than it looks and Britannia metal looks heavier than it feels.

If the novice can be easily fooled over pewter he is on much firmer ground with the metal used for a special sort of cooking pot—the skillet. While the use of the term has been broadened since, the original skillets were three-legged cooking pots made from a specific metal for a very limited time.

Up until the middle of the 17th century church bells were used as a news service as well as summoning the congregation. To support all this merry pealing there was a thriving industry of bell-foundries using metal of a special alloy designed to 'ring true'. When Cromwell and the Puritans came to power they soon put a stop to all that. Joyous peals, along with maypole dancing and

4. A gold and enamel snuffbox, French, circa 1775. It fetched £9,000 in June 1979.

Christmas puddings, were fun, and fun was Sin. So the bells fell silent.

With no welfare state to support them, the bell-founders had to turn to other ways of making a living and one of those was the making of skillets. These pots were designed to stand on the hearth rather than to be suspended above the fire and consequently they had to have very long handles so that they could be thrust into the embers. The bell-founders, being dedicated craftsmen, took great pride in their work and they embellished these long handles with texts or mottoes, and sometimes with initials as well. Cathedrals and churches often have records of the craftsmen who worked on them and it is therefore usually possible—though not easy—to trace the names of the men who cast 17th century bells and to match them with initials on any particular skillet. The moulded texts or mottoes are fascinating indications of the maker's point of view. 'Ye Wages of Sin is Death' may not actually show that the maker was a Puritan himself but at least it is proof that, if he was not, he knew which side to look to for butter on his bread. There can, however, be no doubt about the sentiments of the craftsman bold enough to declare his motto 'Loyal to His Magistie'. Somewhat naturally he was discreetly anonymous.

This use of bell-metal ceased when the bells rang out to welcome

Charles II back to his throne and the bell-makers returned to their proper trade. Three-legged cooking pots did, of course, continue to be made but of baser metal. If in any doubt, lift the pot up. If it is of bell-metal the bottoms of its feet will still be the bright clear pale gold colour however soot-blackened the rest has become. It would be nice to think that it was from the cruder, later pots that the word 'skilly' comes—an abbreviation for skillagallee, the disgusting thin soup dished up to unfortunate prisoners in the hulks in the 18th century.

Skillets can, however, be absolved from any connection with potholes. This word derives from clay pots.

Long before Josiah Wedgwood welded the cottage industries into a cohesive system of manufacture the farmers of Staffordshire used to make crude pottery for their own household needs. They were singularly well placed to do so because in the narrow valley north of Stoke-on-Trent seams of coal and seams of clay ran side by side very near the surface. The inhabitants took full advantage of this freak of geology. The clay was used to make bricks for kilns and the coal was used to heat the kilns. Then it was the turn of clay again, and the coal generated enough heat to bake pots, mugs and plates for the farmhouses.

Before being popped into the kiln the clay had to be compressed. The farmers had no intention of investing in expensive machinery to do the job, especially as plenty of hard-packed clay was available near at hand, or rather near at foot. So, at night when nobody was about, they would sneak off and dig up a spadeful of compressed clay from the tracks which passed for roads in those days, leaving only another declivity in the uneven surface. It is small wonder that the next wayfarer, stumbling into it, should mutter something uncomplimentary about potholes.

It is a far cry from those crude and clumsy lumps of clay to the elegant jardinières which were such a feature of late Victorian and Edwardian gracious living. No fashionable Victorian house was without its conservatory, a romantic glade of palm trees, yuccas, with perhaps a fountain tinkling its spray into a grotto of ferns. The conservatory was just the place to cool off in—or not cool off—in the intervals between plunging about the ballrooom in those vigorous polkas to which the Victorians were much addicted. Supreme among the potted plants reigned the aspidistra, which in due course led the movement away from the conservatory into the Edwardian house itself. Conservatories, those shrines of mystery with their dim lights and distant music have been swept away by the harsher light and brasher sounds of what we are pleased to call progress. Even the aspidistra itself was relegated to the status of a music-hall joke.

But the wheel is coming round again. The music-hall has become something of a music-hall joke and it is the aspidistra which is steadily climbing back into fashion. In fact houseplants in

5. *Marqueterie-sur-Verre* by Gallé.

Plate VII. An elegant jardiniere.

general are making a comeback, so if you secretly think that the aspidistra is a rather dull and unsympathetic plant there are plenty of others to choose from, just as there are containers to put them in. But the best container of all must surely be that designed expressly for the purpose. In company with the houseplant, the jardinière is enjoying a strong and deserved revival. As with all antiques, jardinières vary in aesthetic appeal but one thing they all have in common. They are magnificent examples of the potter's art. The jardinière consists of two pieces, a stand with a bowl on top, and not the least of its attractions is that it is a large and important item in any scheme of decoration. Even a single jardinière can make an entrance hall look furnished, and a pair bestow an air of dignified graciousness.

The heyday of the jardinière was the last quarter of the 19th century and the first quarter of the 20th when leading firms such as Doulton, Minton and Wedgwood produced an enormous number of varieties. A very hard, rough clay was used and the jardinière was coated with cream-coloured slip, fired, then hand-painted and fired again. The colours are beautifully clear and the glaze as fine as you will find on bone china. Perhaps a little overpowering when empty, when softened with a plant, a vase of flowers or trails of

6. Stucco Head of the Buddha. Gandhara-Hadda, 3rd to 4th century.

ivy, a jardinière can look extraordinarily graceful and attractive. Now in high fashion, they cost anything from £200 to £3,000.

Another much smaller type of container which can be used as a flower vase may sometimes be found tucked shamefacedly away at the back of an antiques shop. It is of course well known that much 'Benares' brass was made in Birmingham, but what is not so well known is that at the beginning of this century there was a thriving industry in Cairo making fake funerary urns. They were sold by the boatload to the rich English tourists on their way back from wintering in Luxor, and borne proudly home by people who never questioned that the clearly hand-made and rather battered looking objects had been lying in a tomb since the time of the Pharoahs.

The passage of eighty or a hundred years has added a genuine patina of age to these little things and if you can manage simultaneously to know that they are fakes and to forget this fact they are really quite ornamental and cost very little.

In complete contrast is a type of artefact which looks like a fake and is in fact a genuine antiquity. This is the rare and beautiful tomb ornament from India, dating from the Gandhari period in the 2nd or 3rd century. The reason why one could easily be mistaken for a fake is that the faces are much more European than Indian. In fact one could be forgiven for mistaking the modelling for Grecian, and one would be almost right, for the culture of the Gandhari period shows the very strong influence left behind by Alexander the Great whose conquests extended right into India.

The owners of the little boutiques and the stall-holders have, on the whole, a good all-round knowledge of antiques and a genuine interest in them, otherwise they would be selling cabbages or cigarettes. But their knowledge is seldom sufficiently specialised to recognise a Gandhari tomb ornament and they are quite likely to price at a few pounds an object worth £8,000 or £9,000. It is, admittedly, not very likely that you will come across such a bargain, but what a vindication of the Saturday stroll it would be if you did!

Colour plate by courtesy of Barrie Quinn Jardinières. Figures 1, 2, 3 and 5 by courtesy of Phillips. Figure 4 by courtesy of Sotheby's. Figure 6 by courtesy of Barling of Mount Street.

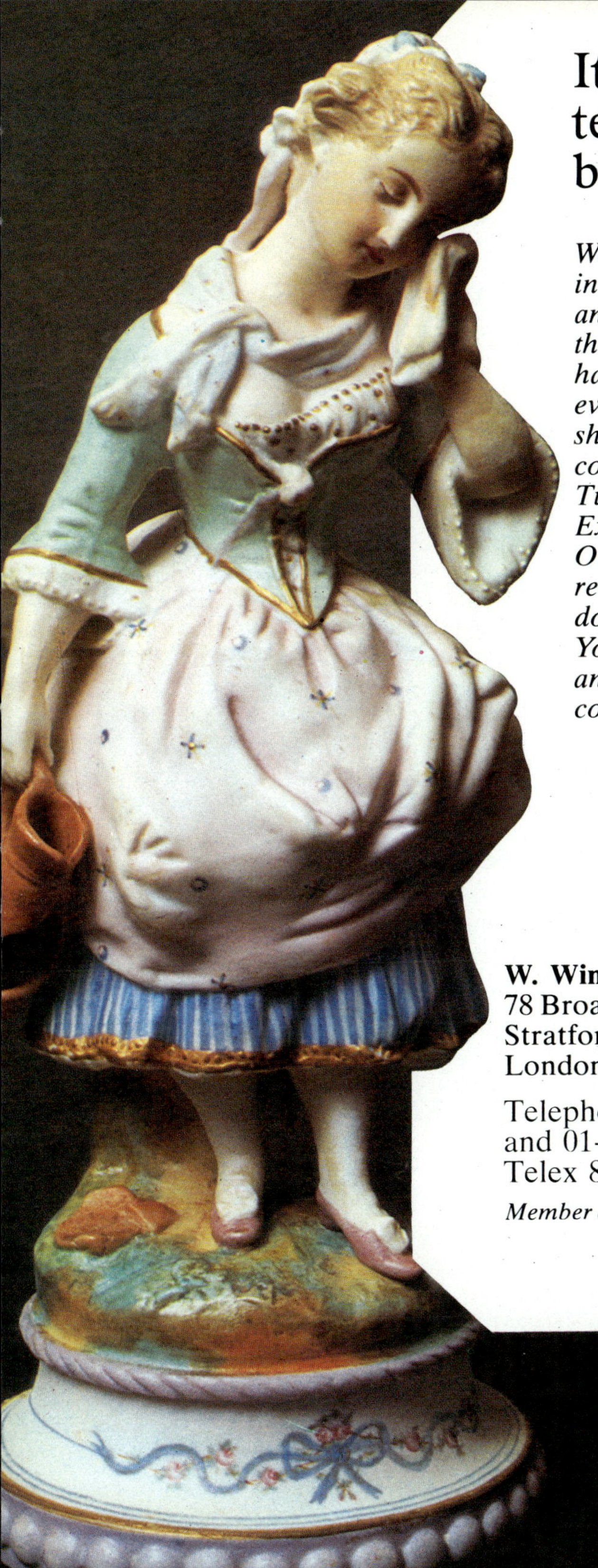

Plate VIII. George III 'Three graces' crown.

CHAPTER EIGHT

Coins

by Robert E. Darley-Doran

Render therefore unto Caesar

St Matthew

GIVEN our knowledge of human nature, it is probable that coin collecting must have started shortly after the first coins appeared from the mints of Aegina and Lydia in the 7th century B.C. In the absence of any clear evidence, however, it is perhaps Croesus, King of Lydia, who should be considered for the honour of being the world's earliest coin collector, for it was he who first struck coins of pure gold from the electrum that was washed down from the mountains which rose behind his capital at Sardis. It would be only natural for Croesus to have saved samples of the best-struck pieces to show to travellers who were eager to see them for themselves and to become familiar with his new invention of money.

Later, as the use of coins spread throughout the Greek world, rich traders and members of the newly-established profession of moneychanger probably kept samples of the coins that were currently in use around the shores of the Mediterranean. Not only would a collection of sample coins from each city state provide a standard of verification, but it would also excite aesthetic appreciation of the high artistic standard set by the die-engravers. Indeed, each state vied with its neighbours in putting its coins to use as religious, cultural and political ambassadors. Today the archaic and classic coinage of ancient Greece is loved for its unselfconscious beauty, which takes the collector back to an age when our civilisation and art was in its first bloom of youth and spontaneity.

It was after the conquests of Alexander the Great that portraits of actual rulers came into use on the coinage. This enabled the coinage of Rome, especially that struck by the emperors, to become a tool of political propaganda of the first importance, because coins were the only means of mass communication available before the invention of printing. The historians of Rome would have found that the possession of a coin cabinet was roughly equivalent to a photographic history of their state. Certainly today there is no more delightful companion to the reading of ancient history than a well-furnished cabinet of coins and medals, for the lifelike portraits of the rulers, their wives and children, and illustrations of their public works, their triumphs and deifications, give a sense of immediacy which no other historical relics can provide.

Although coin collecting ended in Western Europe following the barbarian invasions of the fifth century, it probably continued in the more cultured environment of Byzantine until the sack of Constantinope in 1204. One hundred years later was born the first historically verifiable coin collector, Francesco Petrarch, the earliest of the great humanist figures of the Italian Renaissance. By the time of his death in 1374, Petrarch was probably only one of many cultivated men who were captivated by the coinages of ancient Greece and Rome. It was under their influence that imitation coins and medals began to be struck, and were preserved along with their antique prototypes in the coin cabinets of kings and princes, prelates and amateurs of the arts. Since the Renaissance, coin collecting and its attendant discipline of numismatics have been the object of increasing interest as new fields of collecting have opened to the curious and dedicated.

The natural impulse of a young collector when he is choosing his area of interest propels him towards acquiring a deeper understanding of what is already familiar to him. This is why a London boy will be drawn towards modern British coins as his fellow collectors in Paris, New York and Frankfurt turn to their own national coinages. Most coin shops cater to this type of collecting by selling holders with spaces for each coin type and date which can be filled up as the collection grows. Usually the novice settles upon gathering several common and modestly-priced denominations, fills up the spaces as quickly as his purse will permit, and then, over a longer period, upgrades the pieces in less than perfect condition in order to acquire a series of coins each one of which is in as near uncirculated condition as possible.

Often the youthful collector will let his interest lapse for a time because of other more urgent demands upon his resources. Rare indeed is the young man who places collecting before his social life and the establishment of a family. The ones who do may well end up as bachelors. For some curious reason, men outnumber women as coin collectors by at least a hundred to one, although there are many shrewd women dealers. This may be because collecting is a private act, akin to that of the hunter who goes out alone to stalk his prey, and that it compensates for a thwarted hunting instinct among men. For most of us our serious collecting interests begin when we have a certain amount of surplus cash and time on our hands, when suddenly, often without warning, the urge to assemble a collection comes back.

Collecting then becomes an art and a science which demands constant practice, devotion and study if success is to be achieved. It requires patience and discipline to attain the high degree of skill needed in selecting the right pieces, although trial and error are nearly always present in the initial stages of the work. The first question is to decide what to collect. Many different factors come into play here. For example, what are the best opportunities in the place where the collector lives? How far can he go in satisfying his interests? Are the coins priced so that he can afford to sustain a reasonable rate of growth for his collection? It is natural for the collector to hunt that which he can reasonably expect to find close to home. This is why the youthful tendency to collect what is familiar frequently develops into a preference for the coins of the collector's own country. Generally speaking, both the demand and supply of a particular coinage is greatest in the area where it was originally struck. There are, however, three exceptions to this rule: the classical coinage of Greece, Rome and Islam, and these are collected by people who, regardless of their national origins, have a particular interest in the culture that produced them. None the less, the improvement in communications and the availability of popular coinage handbooks has helped to satisfy the needs of international collectors, and has facilitated the exchange of both coins and information about them to an extent that has never been seen before.

A few observations on coin collecting in general are as follows:—Once the initial fascination with a series has set in, the collector should learn as much as he can about the coins in order to breathe life into his new possessions. This means that the serious collector cannot do without a numismatic library on his subject. He usually starts off by purchasing the popular guide to his chosen series, which gives price indications, rarity tables, production statistics and collecting trends in that particular field. The emphasis in such guides is frankly commercial, and they are prepared by dealers for collectors. As a general rule the better known the series, the more reliable they are, because the price information has been built up over many years and represents the experience of a large number of collectors and dealers. The more advanced collector usually acquires a library of the classic numismatic works on his collecting speciality and on cognate coinage groups. The more important dealers in coins also have well-established departments which buy and sell numismatic libraries.

One should choose dealers as one would the purveyors of any specialised professional service. Reputation is very important to the best of them, and these are the ones to whom a collector should go if he wishes to buy rare coins. The right dealer is one who is an expert on his particular subject, he may well have published his own guide to the series, he has many satisfied clients, a large

Roman. Julius Caesar Silver denarius.

Greek. Silver didrachm of Larissa in Thessaly 400–344 BC.

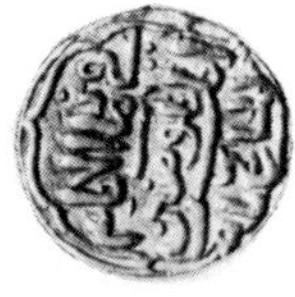

Islamic. Gold Tanka of Muhammad II b. Tughlák 1325–1351.

Byzantine. Justinian I Bronze follis.

English. George II crown 1751.

English. Proof Sovereign 1871.

English. Bank of England Dollar 1804.

English. Edward VI Gold half sovereign.

turnover of material, and is always prepared to stand by the genuineness of his stock. This is especially important if the ever-present danger of counterfeits of rare coins is to be controlled. A large specialist dealer has the opportunity to gain visual impressions of the real article as contrasted to the counterfeit, and he can often prevent fraud by refusing to accept suspect coins and reporting his suspicions to Interpol. The prices charged for coins may vary widely according to the dealer and the locality, and for the commoner pieces it is worth shopping around to find the best buy. The fact that one dealer may sell a coin at £5.00 while another charges £7.50 for a piece in the same condition does *not* mean that the latter is necessarily overcharging; he may have higher overhead costs, or need to meet the extra expenses of maintaining a larger stock of material for his clients. Work closely with your dealers. Exchange information if you are an expert and listen carefully to their advice if you are not. Dealers do have favourite customers, and it well worth the effort to become one of these if you can. Although money helps, it is not the only or the best way to win such favour. Sincerity and knowledge will often give you an insider position which will enable you to purchase a rare coin that might not be shown to everyone. Many of the better dealers take the trouble to learn their clients' particular interests and plan their purchases to fulfil individual collecting needs.

Collect only that which gives you personal pleasure and do not be swayed by passing fashions. Your *own* collecting theme is the right one for you, and if you follow it with persistence and imagination the result will give you a sense of satisfaction for a job well done. This advice is important, because coin collecting should not be viewed as a "get rich quick" scheme. The contemporary boom in collecting is a reflection of world-wide inflation. If price stability should return the inflated profits expected by speculators in coins, stamps and precious metals would not materialise, and values could be expected to drop sharply.

Certain series are much easier to collect than others. For example, anyone can acquire a magnificent series of British coins without too much difficulty if he has enough money to spend on acquiring them. The series is well known to many collectors, there is a constant turnover of coins and the values are relatively well established. Most importantly, enough of the "classic" rare coins have survived to make their acquisition little more than a matter of money and patience. Furthermore, this series provides enough scope to give enjoyment to every degree of collector from those with only modest means to the very rich, and from the financially innocent to the keenest speculator.

Other series may not be so easy. The modern Greek coinage is one such example. Although the state is scarcely a hundred and fifty years old, it would be difficult for more than two or three serious collectors to build up comprehensive collections of the

Greek series. This is not for want of knowledge but for lack of coins; relatively few were struck and fewer good examples were saved by contemporary collectors. Another is the silver and gold coinage of the Umayyad caliphs of Islam. While much of their coinage is common, many issues are known only from unique examples in public or private collections. The likelihood of any collector living long enough or being sufficiently fortunate to find a sample of each issue is virtually inconceivable, especially since new mints and dates frequently come to light.

Minor denominations, while less expensive, are often more difficult to obtain in good condition than are the crown-size coins. Small coins were more frequently used in trade, and therefore a smaller proportion have survived in excellent condition than of the large ones which saw relatively less circulation or were kept by collectors for their artistic interest alone. This tendency is particularly pronounced in the coinages of poor and unsophisticated countries where, in addition to heavy use, many coins were further damaged by being converted into jewellery. Thus it is usually more a matter of sheer collecting persistence and luck than of cash expenditure to build a good collection of minor coins in preference to one of the large, crown-size pieces.

The budding collector should join and support his local and national numismatic societies, and if he has a particular collecting speciality become a member of any club or society that is devoted to his area of interest. Coin collecting, while an individual and private pursuit, is not best carried out in isolation from other collectors. Obviously there is knowledge and fellowship to be derived from those with similar interests to one's own, but perhaps even more importantly, there is the question of preserving or expanding the freedom to collect. Unfortunately in some countries coin collecting comes within the purview of laws governing the sale or export of antiquities or the possession of bullion. If the provisions of the law are too strict or harshly applied, collecting suffers, or in extreme cases even becomes illegal. Numismatic societies can and do perform the important function of representing collector interests to parliamentary and governmental institutions.

Consider the question of rarity. Several different factors may make a coin rare in the eyes of the buyer or seller. The first concerns the isssuing authority. While coins of the United States of America are common, those of the Confederate States of America are rare, as are many emergency coinages struck in time of war or rebellion. If there are many collectors of a cognate coinage group, then the coins of a rare issuing authority become very valuable. If, on the other hand, the rare issuing authority is obscure and the coins are of little artistic interest, the coins would have value only to the numismatist/scholar.

The second is coins which are rare in their type. In this category may be placed many proof, trial and pattern coinages, such as the five-guinea pieces of George III, the U.S. $4.00 Stella gold, the Ottoman-Egyptian 500 piastre gold, and, on a less exalted level, the regular issues of seldom-seen denominations such as the two-sovereign piece or the George V crown. Such rare type pieces are important acquisitions for collectors who need them to complete sets of a particular coinage.

The third category comprises coins which, while they are common in type, are rarely encountered in a particular year of issue. Famous examples include such major rarities as the 1917 George V sovereign struck at the Royal Mint and the 77 A.H. Umayyad dinar of 'Abd al-Malik, which was the first true Islamic coin to be struck. Rare dates are particularly sought after by specialist collectors who wish to acquire a sample of each coin in a series.

The fourth and largest category is coins which are rare in their condition. This is usually understood to mean those coins which are rarely found in new or nearly new condition, but it could equally well be applied to those in used condition, such as modern speculative issues which scarcely ever enter circulation despite their official status as legal tender. Rarity of condition is important to collectors and speculators of otherwise common coins. By paying high prices for beautifully-struck and perfectly-preserved examples of pieces which, if they were in poorer condition practically anybody could buy without much trouble or expense, added interest can be given to a collecting speciality.

Naturally rarity is relative. To the curator of a national coin cabinet or any other numismatic scholar, a coin is rare if only two or three examples are known. To a specialised dealer or collector a coin is rare if he can only obtain a sample in the condition he wants with a fair degree of patient enquiry and a noticeable expenditure of cash.

Attend coin shows and auctions to get the feel of the market. London in particular is the clearing-house for coins in the E.E.C., thanks to the sane regard for collectors and their needs which is exhibited by the laws of the United Kingdom. Because of increased speculator interest, however, the atmosphere of the great trading-houses has lost the leisured air of the pre-inflation era. The influx of new customers has also attracted a class of person which makes better security arrangements an absolute necessity. With coin sales frequently in the news, criminals have been attracted to their worth as coins rather than as bullion. It is therefore wise for the collector to beware of so-called bargains being offered to him by unknown people, and suspicious instances should be reported to the police. Who knows, the next theft might be of one's own collection unless it is properly safeguarded.

All illustrations by courtesy of B. A. Seaby Limited.

LOT 2

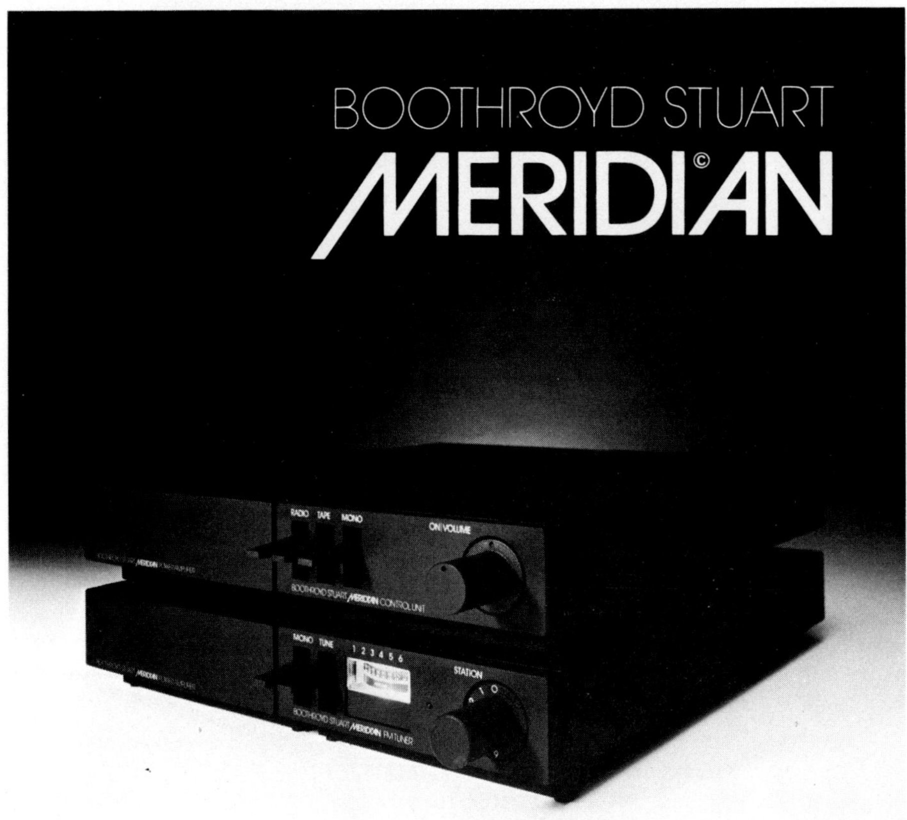
BOOTHROYD STUART
MERIDIAN©
RADIO TAPE MONO
ON/VOLUME
MONO TUNE
1 2 3 4 5 6
STATION

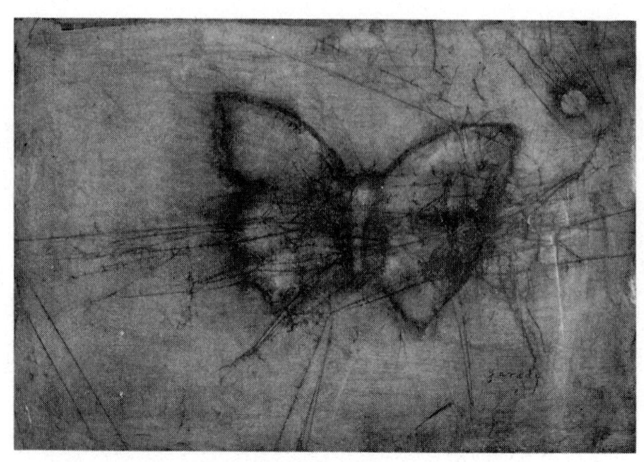

MOON-MOTH

Open are your pale
opalescent wings,
powdered with a silver-green
feathery dust,
as poised
upon a moonlit branch
you rest . . .
bewildered
in your elusive beauty
as though
all other moths
were not grotesque
brown dwarfs
beside
your lunar glow.
The goddess of the moon
from her gilded lantern
bade you flee
To Earth—and thus
   you
      descended . . .
down some cobwebbed shaft,
desiring,
yet ignorant of your desire,
   . . .and now,
with a frightened tremor
of your gossamer frame
you seek once more
the moon . . .
from whence
   . . .you came.

CHAPTER NINE
Antiques of the Future

I hate all Boets and Bainters.

King George I
1660 – 1727

WHILE it is natural to approach the antiques of the remote past with awe and those of the immediate past with nostalgia we must not neglect those of the future. Today's technology requires that much of the individual talent, available just as abundantly as it ever was, is directed into mass creativity. Industrial productivity encompasses what in the past would have been the output of the single artist and craftsman. The genius of one man or woman undergoes such a system of absorption, amalgamation, computerisation and general transmogrification that when it is churned out on the conveyor belt of repetition we do not recognise it as genius at all.

It is, therefore, all the more important to pay attention to those areas of art in which people produce work which is uniquely personal. As representative of two such areas we select painting and poetry as exemplified by the poems of Suzette Childeroy Compton and the paintings of Michael Garady.

We take for granted that if somebody writes a song somebody else will write the music for it, if the writer of the words has not already done so. What is far more unusual is for painting and poetry to be combined, as these two have done. Sometimes it is the painting which inspires the poetry, sometimes the other way round. Each can, of course, be enjoyed separately but it does not diminish either to say that here is a case of the whole being greater than the sum of the parts.

In fact, so closely are the two art forms integrated that one can use almost the same words in describing each. Both have an underlying strength which gives a convincing integrity to the surface delicacy. Both are subtle in their use of emphasis and restraint. They are satisfyingly complementary one to the other.

WAR REQUIEM

Death greets Life
With a spectral smile:
Life greets Death
With insufficient guile
And the one asks the other
If it's all worthwhile

CUCKOO BY MOONLIGHT

Moon-silvered cuckoo
Sleep-flying, floating,
A waterlily
in a moon-drenched dream;
Speechless, songless
Unaware
Of the nightjar's screech
Oblivious
Of the peacock's scream . . .
Nonchalantly letting fall
A moonlit feather
Like a handkerchief
Of frosted lace.
Cognisant
If only in sleep
Of some secret, hidden place . . .
Here—no longer the intruder
Nor harbinger of spring
Better far than any nightingale
The moon-silvered cuckoo
Will . . . of a sudden . . . sing.

THE CONCERT DRESS

Clara Haskil, pianist (1895-1960)

It bears an air forlorn
Black and ivory, long-skirted, plain
So neatly cared for it seems scarcely
To have been worn . . .
We glance towards it, the talisman,
Look away
And, lingering, look again . . .
Would any lesser spirit have left
All the life that now encircles
This strangely hallowed gown?
    . . . to those bereft
It recalls the wearer's joy
Or sorrow . . . her smile . . . her frown.
A simple dress, reminding the world
In its chaste, unworldly way
Of the fingers
That had smoothed it: the genius
Sadly inclined above the keyboard
Hands poised to play
Like a petalfall
Or thunderstorm . . .
    . . . evanescent . . .
Yet still moving on, restlessly, between us
Still amongst us—to this day.

FLOWERS IN A MIRROR

The flower vase stood
on a cloth of crushed velvet . . .
or was it a tray of carved olivewood
and on it, potpourri?
Buds, full-blown heads
of porcelain roses . . . blossoms
embroidered in shimmering threads
or sculpted from silver and gold
into filigree . . .
And now, flowers in a mirror
gazing out in surprise
at their seemingly bold
tangible selves . . . rainwet
calyx, petal and stem:
knowing nothing of their perfumed
forms: bewildered—and yet
somehow half-recognising them,
not understanding their language
of whispers in fragrant flower-scents.
But these, too, in their turn, marvel
at the looking-glass design
as an infant might, each
in their own innocence:
flowers mirrored
thoughts collected . . . combine.

WORLD OF WINDOWS

How cold . . . painful and pained . . .
seems the world
on the other side of this window,
as I look out:
I must try . . . and try again,
to open it, this barrier . . .
but, why,
with all my wrenching
and forcing and shaking,
will it not move?
Please help me
to break those panes of glass
without hurting myself—
or anyone else—
so that I may reach out
and beyond
and breathe more freely . . .
For I feel that if I move on
to the other side—
there
and only there,
will I find the warmth of the sun,
the wild abandonment of space . . .
which is lost to me now . . .
. . . and even as I stand here,
patiently,
with folded arms,
not touching the window
not struggling with it,
not hurling any object against it
. . . suddenly . . .
it cracks—
and every pane of glass
is slowly . . .
. . . shattered . . .
so that there is nothing—
even transparent—
between myself
and the vital freshness of the air
beyond.

THE WIDOW

Lost . . . the terrace broods, quiescent
in a desolate, sea-sprayed dream:
sea-lulled and wind-hushed
and I am lost with it . . . without
your touch.
Moonlight . . . makes the white squares
of a chequered cloth
gleam
like some sea-monster's teeth,
while a ghostly candle weeps
in grey solitude:
its tears
cascade in a profusion
of waxen veils, masking the wreath
of its holder . . .
And so . . .
even each flat, round sea-grape
leaf
seems turned from disc
into far bolder
unknown, chimeric shape . . .
Yet still . . .the terrace broods on,
deep
in a deep-sea trance:
adrift
in a world of black coral and fin,
and I . . . am adrift too,
without sleep
within
another strange world . . . without
you . . .

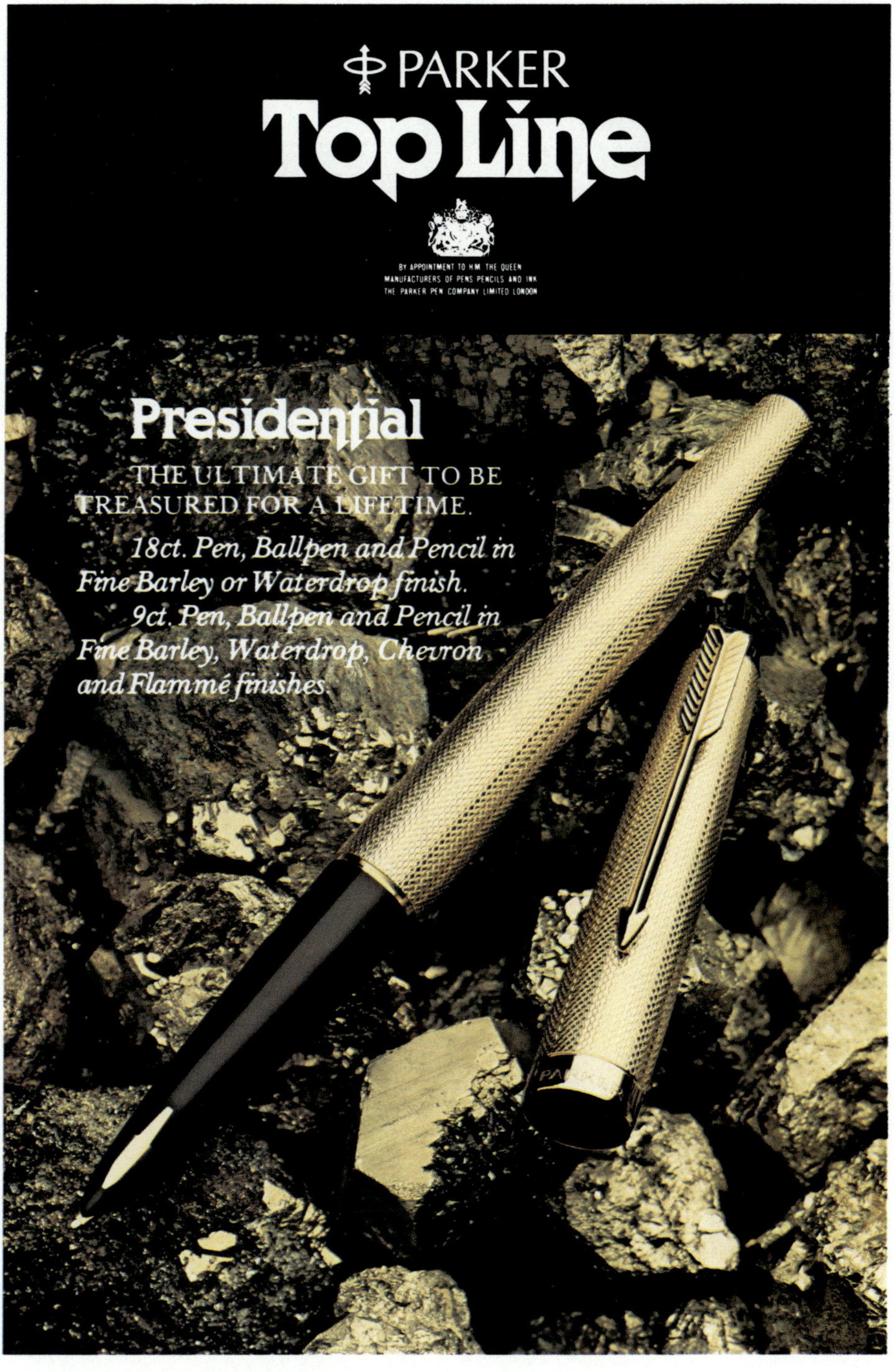
PARKER
Top Line
BY APPOINTMENT TO H.M. THE QUEEN
MANUFACTURERS OF PENS PENCILS AND INK
THE PARKER PEN COMPANY LIMITED LONDON
Presidential
THE ULTIMATE GIFT TO BE TREASURED FOR A LIFETIME.
18ct. Pen, Ballpen and Pencil in Fine Barley or Waterdrop finish.
9ct. Pen, Ballpen and Pencil in Fine Barley, Waterdrop, Chevron and Flammé finishes.

Plate IX. A 1d red, a 1d black and a two penny blue, posted in 1840.

CHAPTER TEN
Stamps
by Robson Lowe

He thought he saw an Albatross
That fluttered round the lamp:
He looked again, and found it was
A penny-postage-stamp . .

Lewis Carroll (Charles Ludwidge Dodgson)
1832 – 1898

MOST of the buyers of postage stamps are collectors, the avid and the casual, the incurable, the wealthy and the poor. These folks are 98% of the buyers. The incurable pays all he can afford, the wealthy what he considers it is worth to him.

The speculator is one who tries to corner the supply hoping that the price will rise. Collectors tend to resent speculators and if his purchases become unpopular with the general collector buyer, then the speculator can lose heavily. Perhaps 4 to 5% of buyers are investors. This category can be divided into the collector investor who spends more than hobby money because he feels that he is both saving and investing, and the investor who just buys stamps that he thinks will rise in value. The investor just described has an immense influence on market prices. Personal knowledge of these buyers shows that the most intelligent buy fine quality stamps of the classic period, often a fairly wide range of subjects based on the belief that fashions of collecting will mean that there is unlikely to be any serious loss, and that the steady growth in the numbers of collectors means that when he wants to sell, demand is generally going to be greater than when he bought.

Then there is the simple investor who concentrates on the simple stamps such as the 20th century high values of Great Britain and the British Empire, the popular commemoratives of the World prior to 1940. With one or two exceptions, the enormous increases in values are confined to such stamps. This is not a healthy demand as a great deal of this merchandise is bought in duplicate. In one extreme example, an investor has bought eighty examples of the Great Britain 1929 P.U.C. £1. In the few years that he has been buying, prices he has paid have varied from £200 to £1,900. A dozen other investors have around twenty copies each of this stamp. All investors have to sell at some time and who is going to buy the several thousand copies of the 1929 £1 when the flood of

Great Britain 1d black 1840.

USA 1847 5c.

USA 1847 10c.

New York 1845 5c.

Columbus 1893 $5.

Great Britain 1913 £1.

USA 1918 24c inverted centre.

Kenya & Uganda 1922 £50.

Cyprus 1928 £5.

selling starts? This is not a stamp in short supply – around 50 to 80 copies come on the market every month and if the investors do not buy them then the price will fall to the figure at which this stamp is attractive to *collectors.* It is sheer guesswork as to what this price will be but judging by the numbers printed, and four out of five are in the hands of collectors and investors, somewhere between £100 and £200 would be the price if investors had not run the stamp up to its present level.

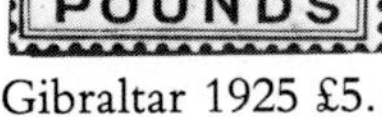

Gibraltar 1925 £5.

Great Britain 1929 £1.

There are plenty of other stamps whose price has been greatly inflated by investor buyers – from Great Britain the ever popular penny black, the 1882 £5, the 1913 £1 being the great favourites. The penny black, first issued in 1840, was the first adhesive postage stamp so almost every collector wants one. Over 60 million were printed and probably between two and five million survive. Some enthusiastic specialists have made specialised collections of this one stamp amounting to two to three thousand examples. Of course a million other collectors ranging from the school-boy to the advanced philatelist would like to own an example but the phenomenal increase in price during the 1978-79 season (160%) was not caused by the genuine collector demand but by a comparatively few investors who decided that a selection of superb examples was better than money. There was a curious recession in the prices for superb examples towards the end of the season when the investors dropped out of the running. The general level of the fine examples remained fairly constant at £100 to £150 but the truly exceptional examples were selling for £220 to £240 instead of £900. As a percentage of the turnover in penny blacks, this recession passed almost unnoticed – the sellers were still getting five to ten times as much as they had paid for them a few years ago

In other fields collectors are fond of the highest values of the Edward VII and George V reigns, stamps with a face value of £5 to £100 and inevitably issued for revenue purposes and not postage, although most of the stamps are inscribed POSTAGE & REVENUE. Such stamps are simple, have always been pricey and are usually the most valuable stamps in that particular colony. Today few real collectors afford an example, for they can get so much more pleasure for their money by buying the less expensive. If the collector is very keen on completeness, he will usually buy the high value overprinted SPECIMEN for a tenth of the price of the normal.

The above words were written before visiting North America in mid September 1979 where I met some two hundred collectors and investors. The healthiest sign in this market is the large number of serious collectors who are following their own particular subject. Of course, I would have met many more investors if it had been my policy to cater for their needs.

While in New York I read a cutting sent to me with an article by Bruce Stone under the general title *Alternatives to Futures – Stamps. Another collectible (sic) alternative.* The writer enumerated what is wrong about stamps – non-income producing, patience is required, fragile, liquidity (difficult to turn into quick cash), etc. He then traced the record of 38 stamps in the American market – 1929 $625, 1939 $970, 1967 $4,500, 1979 $32,000. Exceptional improvement but these are the most popular of American stamps, twenty-five of the 38 being easily subject to defect. One could select less popular U.S. stamps which were practically contemporary where the rate of increase in value was very much less.

Another favourite with the American philatelic investor is the 1918 24 cents Airmail with the centre (aeroplane) inverted of which 100 exist, Myron Kaller reports prices 1940 $4,500, 1964 $15,000, 1969 $31,000, 1974 $47,000, 1977 $60,000, 1979 January $100,000, April $135,000. A block of four of this stamp sold to a syndicate in 1977 for $220,000 has just been resold to a Florida property investor for $500,000.

Back in England for a week, I watched the auction results with keen interest. It was obvious there were plenty of buyers and the turnover in September was up nearly 40%. Last season prices exceeded estimates by 28% with 12.3% of the property offered remaining unsold. All round September prices were 69% over estimate with 15.2% unsold. London October prices were 15.3% over estimates with 32.5% unsold.

So we went over to Switzerland to watch the operations there where prices were averaging 23.8% over estimate with 20% unsold. Here we looked at each group separately – Europe + 14.7%, Balkans and Levant + 14.3%, Great Britain and the Empire + 13.2%, Far East + 77%, Latin America + 52.3%.

What are the investors doing? They are no longer sinking large sums in the high values of Great Britain and the 1929 £1 has fallen to something between £400 and £500 (will the tipsters mention that some of their safe bets have fallen around 70% in four months?). The investors are doubting the wisdom of their bets on the British Empire high values (Cyprus 1923 £1 at £2,000, Gibraltar 1935 £5 at £2,285).

These prices indicate that the buyers have more money to spend than they know what to do with.

Take a long view. The life of a stamp printed in a fast ink on a good quality hand-made paper is estimated at over a thousand years if kept in a temperate climate.

There are stamps just over a hundred years old which are hardly known in their original colour as one of the elements has faded. There are stamps that are less than fifty years old printed in inks with a benzene base which are losing their colour already.

After all, we are all mortal. Death, where is thy sting?

P.S. Last month I spent as much as I should and maybe more on one item for my collection. If I sell it next year, I may lose half my money but I shall have enjoyed many hours as the temporary custodian of my little treasure.

All illustrations by courtesy of Robson Lowe Limited.

1. An early 18th century Venetian chasuble.

CHAPTER ELEVEN
Antique Textiles
by J. D. Mayorcas

. . . will serve to ply
The sampler, and to tease the huswife's wool.
John Milton
1608–1674

THE MOST impressive way to demonstrate the amazing upsurge in interest in antique textiles and tapestries is to state candidly that this chapter would certainly not have been included in any comparable compilation of ten years ago. In the course of this chapter I will attempt to explain the many and varied reasons for this relatively recent phenomenon, and try to set it in the context of historical patterns of taste and fashion. A contributory factor has certainly been the new-found feeling for the crafts, a hankering for the old, simple ways of life, a movement much stimulated by the encroaching impersonality of modern technology and bureaucracy. In the light of this, the ecologists have made much of the pollution of even the very air we breathe, and the underlying feeling of unease—accelerated by the energy crisis—has concentrated our minds back to the gentle, more human values of other ages. The importance of textiles in such context is easy to understand. Their social, aesthetic and economic significance is there to be appreciated. Even from a purely financial standpoint, it seems obvious that for some years textiles had been significantly underpriced, indeed almost ignored.

At first glance, a narrow, specialised field, textiles in fact covers an enormously wide and varied area. In order to give some pattern to any sort of analysis of collecting trends it will be necessary to break up the subject into identifiable areas. One of the most dramatic increases in recent years has been in the price of embroidered samplers; perhaps part of the reason for this is to be found within the general analysis given above, the feeling of social and personal attachment for the little girl who sat at home learning her stitches, her alphabet, and meticulously transposing them on to the canvas in front of her. Of course, simply regarding samplers as signed and dated little pictures of the seventeenth and eighteenth century would suffice—purely commercially—to make them

2. Central detail from a 16th century French bed hanging.

attractive. As historical and social documents they have become important and collectable.

At Christie's South Kensington a sampler dated 1659 made £3,200 some months ago, and this figure was not at all out of the ordinary. Moving further afield, the new wealth of the Middle East has encouraged great interest in embroidered and woven pieces from that area, a trend further stimulated by the current interest in ethnic minorities and tribal movements. Persian, Turkish and Caucasian textiles have become the target for museums and collectors world-wide. Much nearer home, there is a growing demand for English domestic needlework, particularly of the seventeenth century, a period which includes the much sought-after 'stump' or raised work. These naive, almost child-like embroideries blend very well with the simpler, oak furniture now so much in vogue. These charming little pictures were a variation on samplers, and must have been more fun for the children to make because the figures told a story either Biblical or mythological, sometimes with heraldic symbols round the border. Many a little girl must have found the tedium of stitching justified by the result when it took shape as a pussy-like leopard of Braganza (which could date a piece as being made after Catherine of Braganza married Charles II). Another fascinating thing about this peculiarly 17th century form of needlework is that the figures are stuffed with twists of cotton to give the 'raised' three-dimensional effect. A casket covered in raised work made £5,200, also at Christie's South Kensington, in 1978.

It should be mentioned that the general shortage of quality works of art in all fields has led hitherto specialised dealers to venture into new areas, and this, in turn, has led to an upward pressure on prices. Textiles have been much affected by this

Plate X. A French gown, c. 1740. The silk is trimmed with silver lace. In May 1979 it fetched £850.

3. An embroidered cushion, circa 1660. It fetched £420 in February 1979.

4. An 18th century Aubusson tapestry in pastoral style.

movement, fuelled, in turn, by the specialist sales now held regularly at Christie's of South Kensington, Phillips and Sotheby's Belgravia. Museums, too, have played a major role by devoting larger parts of their increased grants to the acquisition of textiles both for display and study purposes. Expanding costume collections have needed new or refurbished premises, and several museums are now in the process of putting this work in hand.

Turning to woven tapestries, the element of fashion has played a large part in determining the enormous variations in prices over the years. It has recently been fashionable to move away from the elegant, sophisticated French eighteenth century weavings to the simpler, more rustic charms of Flemish seventeenth century 'Verdure' tapestries with their restful woodland scenes. With living spaces generally becoming smaller, large panels with mythological or war-like figures have tended to be less popular. The greater spread of knowledge has led to a demand for complete, uncut tapestries, with their original borders, in good state of preservation. Extensive restoration and reweaving is a long and costly business, to be avoided if possible. I remember a cabbage-leaf Flemish 'Verdure' fetching £2,500 in about 1972. This was not considered a particularly low price at the time and yet five years later it fetched £28,000 at auction in Paris.

There are fascinating stories about the market in tapestries over the centuries. In Napoleonic France, for instance, tapestries were confiscated for the value of their gold thread, and what was left was often used for gun-carriage covers. Throughout the nineteenth century, tapestries became increasingly sought after as Victorian 'nouveau riche' entrepreneurs wanted to embellish their richly furnished homes. After the 1929 Wall Street Crash, the market collapsed, and remained depressed until the mid-1930's. During this period, my father had a standing order from a well-known London dealer and decorator to supply him with as many French Hunting-Scene tapestries as he could find. This request was complied with so easily and cheaply that my father was politely asked to sign a declaration that the tapestries were not—to the best of his knowledge—stolen! The war, of course, brought another virtual standstill, but soon after the end, my father was contacted by the head of an international department store chain, and asked if he could locate around one hundred 'Verdure' tapestries for the South American branch. The order was repeated three times, thus virtually emptying Europe of such tapestries. Soon, tapestries were to be fashionable all over the American continent. Naturally, this trend was gradually reversed as dealers from Europe were obliged to cross the Atlantic to look for tapestries to satisfy the new generation of collectors over here. The pattern has more or less evened out now, with demand on both sides of the Atlantic creating a seemingly ever-increasing price spiral that shows no sign of abating.

Perhaps even more notable have been the fluctuations in the demand and price for woven silks; at one time sold at public auction in bundles of twelve, disposed of almost by weight, these beautiful and costly-to-produce weavings are once again beginning to assume their true worth. These rich and decorative textiles have been very much the victims of the vacillations in taste and fashion. The nineteenth century saw a mode for removing original damask

5. An 18th century Aubusson tapestry in Chinoiserie style.

or brocaded coverings from upholstered furniture and recovering with Spanish leather. In the same way, original tapestry-woven chair-covers were discarded of no interest. Just to obtain something for these rejected pieces of tapestry, enterprising dealers made little cushions out of them, and sold them to big stores for a few shillings each. These same little cushions today are avidly collected by dealers, decorators and private clients all over the world, and can run into hundreds of pounds each. The more thoughtful and purist trends in today's thinking have led informed collectors to appreciate the benefits in trying to upholster antique furniture with contemporary textile coverings. The appropriate needlework, tapestry, velvet or woven silk not only brings an effect of harmony that is pleasing to the eye, but also increases the intrinsic originality and thus value of the furniture. Expensive modern fabrics with their harsh chemical dyes seem to detract from, rather than add to, the mellowness of an old chair or settee.

The rise in demand for Oriental carpets is well-known and discussed in another chapter in this book. Within the limited scope of European tapestry-woven or needlework floor-coverings interesting changes of taste have been in evidence. In line with the movement against grand and sophisticated decoration, there has been a tendency away from the chic, delicate Aubusson tapestry carpets, with their pale silky colours and poor record of durability. This movement also underlines the difficulty and expense of good restorations. At the same time, there has been a corresponding increase in popularity (and thus, price) of the more durable, robustly colourful needlework carpets of the nineteenth century, with their bold, no-nonsense floral designs. At the other end of the time scale, the general swing to simpler, less ornate furnishing has meant a much greater interest in oak, thus encouraging a demand for complementary textile embellishments. Plush Spanish and Italian velvets and ecclestiastical embroderies have been much sought after in this context. Their warm tones do much to soften and lighten the dark rigidity of Renaissance or early Baroque furniture. In such settings, it is easy to understand the fashion for English crewelwork embroidery of the Carolean period, with its colourful 'Tree of Life' pattern and rustic, linen-twill background. Until recently a set of crewel stitch curtains would fetch from £500 to £2,000 per pair, according to quality and condition. But suddenly, in the summer of 1979, a set ran up to £8,000 at Christie's South Kensington. Equally in vogue are the small Elizabethan-period needlework bed valances with their elegantly-clad noblemen set against lyrically English country scenery. Gothic and early Renaissance tapestry panels—particularly of small dimensions—are popular and expensive for much the same reasons. An added attraction of these very early pieces is their suitability for use within an ultra-modern decorative setting. Nothing looks more at home in a suede and chrome room than a fifteenth-century tapestry panel.

Thus, in general terms and making due allowance for the vagaries of taste and fashion, it can be stated that antique textiles have far outstripped the recent and current inflation rates and look certain to do even better in the foreseeable future. Taking price levels as they stand today, there is still scope for certain pieces to reach the giddy heights achieved in the 1920's, when dealers of the calibre of Lord Duveen were forming the great collections in the United States. What sets textiles apart from all other kinds of antiques is that they were often cut up and used either for upholstery or some other decorative purpose, particularly in the periods when they were out of fashion. Once this has happened, of course, a piece is either completely lost, or, at best, no longer in its original form. The natural antiques law of constantly diminishing supplies is only too valid in the case of textiles.

To sum up, the rediscovery of textiles as both an enhancement to one's home, and a sound hedge against monetary instability, seems solidy based, emanating as it does from the general public, thence through the activities of dealers and auction houses, and finally reflected in the increased concentration on this field by museums and art collections all over the world. Speculating about the future is obviously a hazardous affair, but it looks sure that small, uncut tapestry panels of the seventeenth century and earlier must continue to rise steadily until their price is somewhere near that obtained by comparable Old Master paintings. Decorative

6. A sampler, signed and dated 1820.

early needlework (particularly English), including 'artefacts' such as stumpwork, mirrors and caskets, is also likely to increase steadily. More dramatic may be the upswing in prices for early samplers, and narrowly specialised areas such as eighteenth century brocaded silks, and woven materials generally. Should Middle Eastern interest—and funds—remain high, embroidered and woven textiles from the indigenous regions, such as Persia, Turkey and Syria, are set to continue on an upward path. European needlework carpets, too, look likely to become more sought-after, though the flimsier Aubusson tapestry-woven floor coverings may well be moving out of fashion. It needs to be stated that any broad generalisations about future trends are always liable to contradiction by pieces which, by their own superior quality or rarity, elevate themselves into a more inflated price range than might be expected. Factors such as acute and ever-increasing shortages, coupled with the rebirth of public and private enthusiasm and the world-wide decline of confidence in paper currencies look certain to propel the value of antique textiles to new and unbreached levels.

Colour plate and Figures 2, 3, 4 and 6 by courtesy of Phillips. Figure 1 by courtesy of Bonham's. Figure 5 by courtesy of Sotheby's.

James Bourlet know all about handling fine art.

Since 1828, the international transportation of fine art has been our speciality – a service as priceless as many of the works of art that are entrusted to our care.

The James Bourlet service is total.

It covers import and export. We have a fleet of vehicles operating in the UK, a scheduled European transport service covering 14 major cities, and fine art consolidation to most international centres.

We have a worldwide reputation for our packing skills and we know which modes of transport to select and recommend, depending on consignment and destination.

We undertake all documentation and, where it is required, we arrange insurance cover.

Such skills and knowledge can only stem from extensive experience. The reputation and integrity of James Bourlet is respected throughout the world.

Picture frame makers

We have a team of highly skilled craftsmen producing a wide variety of superb frames. In addition we apply our wealth of experience to the repair of picture frames and the restoration of paintings to their original condition.

3 Space Waye, Feltham, Middlesex TW14 0TY. Telephone: 01-751 1155.
Telegrams: Titian Feltham. Group Telex: 935242.

26a Conduit Street, London W1R 9TA. Telephone: 01-493 0621.

263 Fulham Road, Chelsea, London SW3 6HY. Telephone: 01-351 3292.
Telegrams: Titian London SW3.

International Transporters and picture frame makers to the art world.

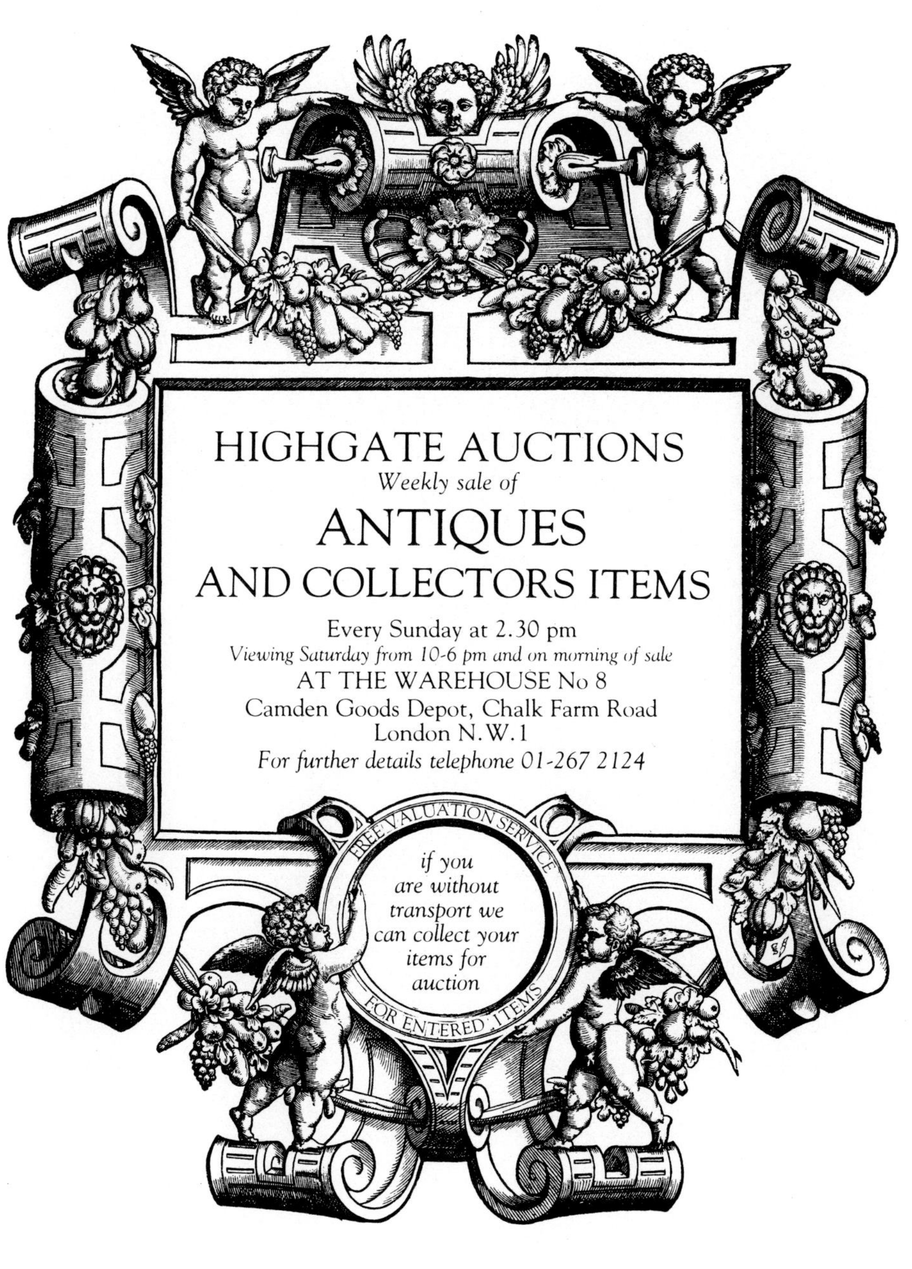

HIGHGATE AUCTIONS
Weekly sale of
ANTIQUES
AND COLLECTORS ITEMS
Every Sunday at 2.30 pm
Viewing Saturday from 10-6 pm and on morning of sale
AT THE WAREHOUSE No 8
Camden Goods Depot, Chalk Farm Road
London N.W.1
For further details telephone 01-267 2124
FREE VALUATION SERVICE
if you are without transport we can collect your items for auction
FOR ENTERED ITEMS

Plate XI. Thomas Gainsborough. John and Henry Truman-Villebois, in a private collection.

CHAPTER TWELVE

Paintings I
Before the Impressionists

by Jeffery Daniels

I want to know a butcher paints

Robert Browning
1812 – 1889

THE GAP between art historians on the one hand and art dealers on the other is nowhere wider than it is in Britain, where snobbish assumptions of superiority over anything connected with 'trade' not only survive, but seem to permeate the art world: the British Museum's refusal to lend to a scholarly exhibition at Agnew's of watercolours by Turner is symptomatic. In the same way, and to an even greater extent, art historians are totally out of touch with popular taste, in so far as this may be gauged by prices paid at auction for particular schools of painting. This is, admittedly, uncertain ground, since other elements, notably the 'investment' syndrome, play their part, but this is more likely to reflect current trends than to influence them. A perfect instance is provided in the period under review by the record prices paid for Dutch and Flemish pictures, whose popularity over the last couple of years was mentioned to me by both Julian Agnew of Agnew and Sons and Andrew Bowyer of Phillips, an auction house that, together with Bonham's is increasingly attractive to the private collector, in search of interesting items at a price he or she can afford.

Nevertheless, Sotheby's and Christie's obviously dominate the field and indeed it was in the latter's London rooms that a world record for a picture by Jan Breughel the elder was established in June 1979: his 'Wooded river landscape with numerous peasants and travellers outside a village', signed and dated 1616, fetched £400,000. There were at least five painters in the family and of this one Peter and Linda Murray, in their *Dictionary of Art and Artists* (Penguin Books, revised ed. 1968) say, somewhat superciliously: 'He was a successful painter of still-life and landscape in a highly detailed style which elicited much admiration from contemporaries. His chief claim to fame is the fact that Rubens collaborated with him.' The work in question has a most

1. Bacchus and Ariadne, by Guido Reni. Los Angeles County Museum.

distinguished pedigree, having belonged in the 18th century to the Elector Karl Theodor of Bavaria and, more recently, to the shadowy and enigmatic Hans Mettler whose beneficiaries sent it for sale, together with 28 other pictures from an amazing collection, virtually unrecorded, which also included a monumental Toulouse-Lautrec, 'La Grande Loge' of 1897, which made another record three days later, going for £370,000. The Mettler Breughel is, characteristically, painted on copper which gives his pictures that richness suggested by his usual appelation of 'Velvet' Breughel: another picture with the same support, a 'Still-life of Flowers' was sold in New York in the previous January for $410,000 (£200,000). At one time the property of Joseph

Bonaparte, King of Spain, it was catalogued in his posthumous sale in the USA (whither he had fled incognito) as Jan van Os but, as Brenda Auslander recounts in *Art at Auction: the year at Sotheby Parke Bernet 1978-79* (ed. Diana de Froment), when it was sent to the salerooms it was recognised as 'typical of Breughel's work'.

Breughel died in 1625 in Antwerp, where five years earlier, Peter Paul Rubens had carried out one of his most important commissions for the Jesuit Church, adorning the ceilings of the side aisles and galleries with a total of 39 paintings on canvas. All were destroyed by fire in 1718, but fortunately numerous sketches by Rubens survive, one of which, 'Saint Clara of Assisi displaying the Pyx on a hilltop above the camp of the Saracens' was sold at Christie's in December 1978 for £60,000, and purchased on behalf of the City of Antwerp. The most spectacular transaction involving works by Rubens was however negotiated privately, by the Heim Gallery in London, on behalf of the National Museum of Wales, Cardiff, which acquired four huge cartoons for tapestry illustrating episodes from 'The Story of Aeneas', probably executed about 1630, for a Roman patron. If their provenance remains a mystery, their importance is unquestionable and their acquisition for Cardiff is a remarkable coup for the recently appointed Keeper of Art, Dr Peter Cannon-Brookes. He was formerly at the City Museum & Art Gallery, Birmingham, which managed to acquire during the year Giovanni Bellini's 'Madonna and Child enthroned', also by means of a private treaty sale, negotiated by Christie's for £400,000, considerably less than half the estimated market value.

Some sales take place in less happy circumstances, and one of the saddest dispersals in recent years was that of the St Albans collection, which included a remarkable depiction of 'Charles II's coronation procession', painted by Roderigo (Dirck) Stoop in 1662: fortunately it has been acquired (through Roy Miles) by the Museum of London. It shows the restored monarch (from whom the Dukes of St Albans are descended, through Nell Gwynne) riding in procession on 22 April 1661, the day preceeding his coronation, from the Tower to Westminster, through a series of triumphal arches. The design for one of these, by Peter Mills, still survives in the RIBA Library. Born in Utrecht, Stoop went to Lisbon, whence he travelled to London in the suite of Charles II's bride, Catherine of Braganza, remaining in England until 1678, when he returned to Utrecht, where he died some five years later. His slightly younger contemporary, Jan van de Cappelle, from Amsterdam, specialised in 'calm seas with fleecy white clouds', and a superb example of precisely these effects, 'Estuary in a calm with pinks, kaags and a States Yacht at anchor' made another record price at Christie's, where it sold for £510,000.

Not everything happens at the two main auction houses however, and one of the most remarkable discoveries of the year under review was made at Bonham's where in July 1978 a tiny painting on copper, whose pre-sale estimate was £150 – £300, fetched £50,000. It had been recognized by Jack Baer of Hazlitt, Gooden and Fox, as one of the predella panels of an altarpiece painted about 1603-05 by Adam Elsheimer. He was a German artist who spent the last ten years of his short life in Rome, where he died in 1610, lamented by Rubens, who deplored the sloth that prevented him from fully exploiting his talent, which was principally for exquisite landscapes peopled by small-scale figures. He always worked on copper and the rediscovered panel is no exception, although, like the other elements of the altarpiece, the metal had been silvered before painting, a fact which helped to establish its origin.

The altarpiece has now been almost completely reassembled at the Stadelscher Kunstinstitut, Frankfurt, where Elsheimer was born in 1578: Mr Baer's panel, representing 'The laying of the Cross upon a sick man' having been re-united with its fellows, only one other piece, again a predella panel, remains to be found, most probably in England, where most of the others have turned up at various times. It has been suggested that the 'Frankfurt Tabernacle' as it is called, which was bought by the Grand Duke of Tuscany in 1619, may later have belonged to the Earl of Arundel, the first real collector in England, whose example stimulated Charles I to build up the Royal collection so that it became one of the most celebrated in Europe. Among the works sold after his execution by the Puritans was a charming panel by Ciulio Cesare Procaccini representing 'The Madonna and Child with the infant St John the Baptist and attendant angels', which came up at Christie's in December 1978, when it went for £150,000, in spite of the fact that it appeared to have been at one time cut down and then enlarged again later.

In his exhibition catalogue *Lombard Paintings* (1974), Peter Cannon-Brookes dates this picture about 1612, a date which has also been proposed for a much larger work by Procaccini that has been sold by Colnaghi's to the Metropolitan Museum New York, a 'Madonna and Child with Saints Francis and Dominic', originally from a church near Milan, where he spent much of his life. The influence of the works of Correggio and Parmigianino is evident in another of his pictures sold by Colnaghi's, to an American museum, 'The Holy Family with St John the Baptist', which has gone to the William Rockhill Nelson Gallery of Art and Mary Atkins Museum of Fine Arts, Kansas City (Missouri). The canvas is again very large, but the figures themselves are also large in scale, although they are painted with Mannerist elegance; the elaborate hairstyle of the Madonna is virtually identical to that of St Catherine in the 'Mystical Marriage of St Catherine' (Milan, Brera) exhibited at Birmingham in 1974, and which Cannon-Brookes dates•to 1612-14. The composition is also remarkable,

2. The Bacino di San Marco, Venice. By Antonio Canale, called Canaletto.

particularly the almost musical disposition of the hands which virtually encircle the Baptist's head.

Such elaboration of gesture is far from the statuesque simplicity of Guido Reni's 'Bacchus and Ariadne', which has recently gone to the Los Angeles County Museum from Viscount Scarsdale's collection at Kedleston Hall, Derbyshire (where it was noted by Horace Walpole in 1765) through Agnew's. It in fact dates from about 1619-20, therefore only a few years later than the Procaccini and the tremendous difference in approach is an indication of a revolution in taste of which Rome and, especially Bologna, were centres and for which the Carracci were principally responsible. In his last years, Reni's manner became looser and more sketchy as can be seen in the 'Moses and Pharaoh's Crown' which the National Gallery of Scotland has acquired, also through Agnew's, and which must date from just before his death in 1642. The influence of Guido Reni was discerned by a contemporary commentator in the important 'Adoration of the Shepherds' by Paolo de Matteis, purchased by the Virginia Museum of Fine Arts, Richmond (Virginia) through the Heim Gallery, which exhibited the work in the summer of 1978. Curiously enough, the pendant to it, an 'Annunciation', passed through the same hands five years ago, and is now also in the USA, in the St Louis Art Museum: both pictures are signed and dated 1712 and were painted in Naples for the Duchess of Laurenzano, later passing to Prince Henry of Bourbon-Parma, whose first wife was a daughter of the last King of Naples, Francis II.

Although Paolo de Matteis was patronized by the Earl of Shaftesbury (for whom he painted the 'Choice of Hercules', now

3. The children of John Angerstein M.P., by Sir Thomas Lawrence. Berlin Picture Gallery, Dahlem.

at Temple Newsam, which is also dated 1712), England's links were closer with Venice than Naples and the arrival of two Venetian ambassadors in 1707 was an occasion of great pomp and pageantry which was recorded by the Udinese painter Luca Carlevarijs in a picture which was lent to the *London and the Thames* exhibition in 1977 by Colnaghi's, who have now sold it to the Alte Pinakothek in Munich. A brilliantly painted work of outstanding interest it should obviously have gone to the National Gallery, which has nothing by Carlevarijs, although the Birmingham City Museum and Art Gallery does possess the companion picture, 'The

4. First Class, by Abraham Solomon, 1854.

arrival of the Earl of Manchester in Venice', which took place in the following year.

Carlevarijs never came to England, but his more famous follower and rival, Antonio Canale, known as Canaletto, of course did, although this was not until 1746 when his manner had begun to acquire that dryness and tightness which give his later pictures a somewhat mechanical quality. His earlier pictures, however, have a freshness and imagination that raises them above the mere recording of places and buildings. A magnificent example comparable with the National Gallery's 'Stonemason's Yard' has also gone to Germany (Stuttgart) through Colnaghi's: entitled 'At Dolo on the Brenta', it must date from 1730 or soon after. The brilliant colours and its excellent condition make it one of the finest Canalettos to have come on the market in recent years, and distinctly superior to the version in the Ashmolean Museum, Oxford. Good examples of his later manner do nevertheless command high prices: a spacious 'Bacino di San Marco' fetched £120,000 at Sotheby's in November 1978, while a 'View of Greenwich from the River with numerous vessels' painted during his English visit, made £140,000 in June 1979 at Christie's.

A different view of the Thames, upstream at Richmond, by the English landscape painter Richard Wilson, has been acquired by the Alte Pinakothek in Munich through Agnew's, who have also sold two major late works by Thomas Gainsborough during the period under review. Manchester City Art Gallery's enterprising new Director, Timothy Clifford has added 'A Peasant girl

5. Spring, by Burne-Jones.

6. An Intercepted Correspondence, by John Frederick Lewis, 1869.

gathering faggots in a wood' to that distinguished collection, now imaginatively re-hung, while the delightful 'John and Henry Truman-Villebois' has been acquired by a British private collector. The freedom of handling, especially in the landscape background, contrasts with the rather studied pose of the two boys, great-grandsons of the brewer Ben Truman, building a house of cards on the steps of a garden temple. Another group, 'The Children of John Angerstein, M.P.', by Sir Thomas Lawrence is a major rediscovery by David Posnett of the Leger Gallery from whom it has been bought by the Berlin Picture Gallery, Dahlem. The children's grandfather was John Julius Angerstein, whose collection of paintings formed the nucleus of the National Gallery, being acquired for the nation after his death at the instigation of Lawrence, who had painted him on several occasions. The 'Mr and Mrs John Julius Angerstein' now in the Louvre (exhibited at the National Portrait Gallery at the *Sir Thomas Lawrence* exhibition 1979-80) shows him with his second wife, and was exhibited at the Royal Academy in 1792, while the Leger picture was exhibited there in 1808. Mr Posnett's discovery (in New York, incidentally) would seem to invalidate the claim of another picture by Lawrence in the Louvre to represent the Angerstein children, since the ages do not fit the date, whereas those in the Berlin picture tally perfectly. The rich colouring, especially the red velvet suit of the boy on the right and the dramatic landscape background confirm the attribution to Lawrence, and it is a pity that it could not have been included in the National Portrait Gallery's exhibition.

The most famous foundling in history was undoubtedly Moses, whose 'discovery', carefully prepared by his mother, has inspired countless artists, from Veronese through Johann Liss to Sebastiano Ricci and G. B. Tiepolo, whose version in Edinburgh is probably the most splendid in all painting. An unusual and highly decorative treatment by the French painter Antoine Coypel (1661-1722) first exhibited in 1699, has recently been acquired from the Heim Gallery by the Allen Memorial Art Museum, Oberlin College (Ohio). Although entitled simply a 'Finding of Moses', it actually depicts the dramatic moment when Pharaoh's daughter chooses the baby's mother as his wet-nurse, which gives the work great psychological and narrative appeal in addition to its considerable pictorial qualities. It shows remarkable discernment on the part of the museum's trustees that they should add such a work to their collection, as the field of French academic history painting is almost totally neglected outside France, with the notable exception of the Heim Gallery, which is in any case of Parisian origin. Another Heim picture, the much later (1761) 'Offrande a l'Amour' by Carlo Vanloo (1705-65) has also gone to the U.S.A., to the Wadsworth Atheneum, Hartford (Conn.): discovered since the 1977 exhibition devoted to the artist in his birthplace, Nice, it is one of the first manifestations of the 'goût grec' and was painted for Madame Geoffrin.

Academic pictures of the 19th century are generally more popular than those of the 'ancient regime', since their content tends to be easier to understand, being anecdotal rather than allegorical or mythological. The enormous price paid for John Frederick Lewis's 'An intercepted correspondence, Cairo' (1869), £220,000 at Christie's in May 1979, is discussed by Philip Hook in *Christie's Review of the Season 1979* (ed. John Herbert), where he forecasts that it will not be long before the best Victorian paintings "reach the Old Master League for prices".

Old Master drawings sometimes command much higher prices than paintings: last season Sotheby's sold a black chalk drawing by Goya for £62,000, while at Christie's a charming red, black and white chalk drawing of his son by Jean Etienne Liotard fetched only £2,000 less. Prints too are in demand, although rarity would seem to be the decisive factor rather than aesthetic appeal: a singularly unattractive South German engraving of c. 1450-65 of 'St Augustine and the child' went for an astonishing £23,000, presumably reflecting the German tendency to buy back their own productions.

Colour plate by courtesy of Agnew's. Figure 2 by courtesy of Sotheby's. Figures 4 and 5 by courtesy of Roy Miles Fine Paintings. Figure 6 by courtesy of Christie's.

Plate XII. La Bouteille de Vin, painted by Pablo Picasso in 1925.

CHAPTER THIRTEEN
Paintings II
Impressionists and After
by Michael Pick

Harriet, Hi!
Light of my eye!
Come to the pictures and have a good cry,

Alan Patrick Herbert
1890 – 1971

ON NOVEMBER 5th 1979 Sotheby's Parke Bernet New York sold a painting by the Surrealist Man Ray of a giant pair of lips apparently poised with intent over the Los Angles skyline. At £360,000 it has proved to be the highest price yet paid for a Surrealist work, surpassing even the prices paid for work by Dali. As an aside, it was noted that the artist had, for some years, used it as a headboard for his bed.

Three days later the same house sold Cezanne's *Paysage en Provence* for £266,666. It came from the collection of Paulette Goddard Remarque who is reported to have said that she could no longer face the responsibility of owning such masterpieces.

Both sales reflect shifts and facets of the market for Impressionist and Modern Art. Prices for works of originality and quality continue to rise to dizzy and hitherto unsuspected heights, something not true of Contemporary Art at the moment. Definition of terms may be helpful here. Impressionism merges into Post-Impressionism with the later work of such artists as Renoir, Monet, Degas and Pissaro which begins to overlap with Cezanne, Gaugin, van Gogh or Seurat, all very different in their techniques but clearly of a certain epoch.

The term Modern Art is mainly applied to the product of the period between the two World Wars although having its roots in the years immediately before 1914. Some painters of this school were of course still active into the 1950s and beyond but generally their styles changed and developed. Contemporary Art is the nomenclature embracing all work from the Second World War up to the present day.

What is of particular interest to British buyers is that there are many burgeoning areas of British and international art which are still relatively inexpensive, offering a variety of choice to the discerning collector.

For those in love with gorgeous colour, texture, light and subtle brushwork the Impressionists work is irresistable. Sotheby's sale on July 4th, 1979 of 'Important Impressionist and Modern Paintings' contained an outstanding work by Renoir 'Le Pêcheur à la Ligne' in which blue and green tones form a typically lush setting for a tender country scene, the white clad woman reading a newspaper, the fawn-clad man intent on his fishing. Renoir saves the scene from banality by giving it a lively sparkle in such touches as the red decoration of the woman's hat and the man's boater. This sold for £610,000, and is also of historic interest as it was bought by the collector Georges Charpentier (for 180 francs) at the famous Hotel Drouot auction in March 1875, when the Impressionists banded together to gain both artistic and financial recognition. Appreciation of quality of talent and artistic skill has of course changed, but the faith which the Impressionists had in the work of each other is endearing: they were sure of themselves and fought for each other. In his auto-biography *Souvenirs d'un Marchand de Tableaux* Ambroise Vollard, the first great dealer in such paintings, gave examples of this. He told how the piecing together of the mutilated 'Execution of Emperor Maximillian' was undertaken by Dégas, intent on rescuing the pieces from such bizarre places as under beds, and all under the fierce control of the artist's widow. Renoir praised the complete work "It is pure Goya and yet Manet was never more himself than in this picture". Manet's 'The Old Musician' was considered unsaleable at the time: the wife of a Conseiller Génèral wanted to buy the picture for the children in the centre and said that she would have just the children, named a sum and took the ensuing silence of Madame Manet to indicate consent. As the woman approached the picture with a pair of scissors Madame Manet suddenly found herself with scruples, blocking the woman's path and shouting, "No, no! Why, it's as if you're murdering my husband." His 'Jeune Fille Lisant, de profil' of 1880, a small brush and india ink sketch, fetched £1,800 at a Sotheby's sale of modern drawings and water colours on July 5th, 1979. Such is the changing taste and attitude that for £80,000 one could have bought Degas' 'Danseuses dans les culisses' a delightful study in muted tones, highlights springing at the eye from the portrayal of the dancers flesh. Two highlights of the year in art sales were the Sotheby sale on July 3rd of Modern Pictures from the Paul Rosenberg Collection, and a day earlier Christie's held the sale from the Mettler Collection of Impressionist and Modern Pictures. Rosenberg was a dealer in the works sold at Sotheby's, which included some fine Picasso drawings, particularly from the period 1918-1919. Two "Pierrots' of 1918 fetched £18,500—and £14,000—respectively and a particularly fine pencil 'Le Pêcheur' £45,000. With all the acclaim heaped on Picasso in his later years one can forget just how fine a graphic artist he was, again the quality commands the price and a

1. Danseuse à la Barre by Edgar Dégas. Drawn circa 1885, charcoal heightened with white chalk. Sold in July 1979 for £15,000.

pen and ink 'Trois Danseurs en repos' of 1925 is an outstanding example with a marvellous sense of rhythm and movement in the lines. It sold for £56,000. His work in oils such as the famous 1925/6 'La Bouteille de vin', a work of bold abstraction and colouring, sold well, in this case for £460,000 (with the 10% premium on top). Thirty-four works of Picasso were included in this sale, each covetable, and none more so in my eyes than 'Nu assis s'essuyant le pied' of 1921 from his classical phase, executed unusually in pastel. This large lady, selling for £280,000, is a precursor of those ecstatically abandoned giantesses bounding across the front curtain (now at the V. & A.) painted for the Diaghilev Ballet 'Le Train Bleu' of 1924.

Ballet and stage designs or illustrations are now an established area of the art-market, yet one still capable of exploration by the non-millionaire. Many of the celebrated works, such as the curtain mentioned above, are expensive and hard to come by, but work by such as George Barbier is both good and collectable. His 'Nijinsky as the Favourite Slave in Cléopâtre', a pen, indian ink and water-colour of 1913, sold at Sothebys on June 6th 1979 for £2,700. Work by Benois, Bakst or Erté has long been known, but there are others less well known, such as Alastair (Hans Henning von Voight) worthy of study. Alastair was a Baltic baron living in Paris during the 1920s, a mixture of Huysmans, Wilde and Beardsley, even during the Jazz Age an eccentric producing intense drawings, for the Black Sun Press of Harry Crosby in particular. There is also much British work to be inspected. Ballet began to make its firm beginnings here in the late 1920s, by the 1930s there were notable stage and ballet productions with sets and costumes by such as Oliver Messel, Rex Whistler or John Piper, a Duncan Grant 'Swan Lake' in 1932, a Vanessa Bell designed 'High Yellow' and there were also the productions designed by Leslie Hurry and Cecil Beaton. British art of this period is curiously undervalued in its native country, and the wealth of material available should prompt collectors.

Still with British art of the period, on the 5th June 1978 'Our Mutual Friend the Horse' a self portrait by Munnings with his wife on horseback, was the star piece of a Christie's house sale. It fetched £36,464, a fair price for a fine painting, but the sale was in America at Ravenscliff, Pennsylvania, and was their second house sale there. This price reflects the steady world-wide interest in Munnings, as a painter of horses. In an ill-lit corridor at Lancaster House hangs a large portrait of 'Anna Pavlova' caught in a moment as 'The Dying Swan.' In spite of its impossible location the luminous quality of the work and sheer vitality of the subject leap at the eye. It is by Sir John Lavery, between the wars a respected academician with an elegant studio in Kensington and a distinguished salon run by his glamorous wife, Hazel, a famous political hostess. His work is literal and a touch romantic, now

2. Léon Bakst at Martychkino Station. Drawn by Alexandre Benois and sold for £5,000 in June 1979.

3. Le Pêcheur. Drawn by Pablo Picasso in 1918.
4. Pierrot drawn by Pablo Picasso in 1918 and sold in July 1979 for £14,000.

unfashionable, and his technique superb. He has none of the bravura of Lászlo, or the rather flashy quality of Boldini nor the lushness of Sargent, he has enormous power to suggest the sitters' character rather than their outer shell. Whilst Contemporary Art is clearly being questioned (the sale results are proving this) a re-assesment of the art of the inter-war years in England should follow. The 'Thirties' exhibition at the Hayward Gallery from 25 October 1979 to 13th January 1980 is a beginning. Victorian painting has been re-assessed and popularised with exhibitions for similar reasons. The work of the Camden Town Group is already well known through Sickert, Gilman's work is increasingly popular, but there others such as the later Euston Road school and then there are Laura Knight, selling fitfully, Orpen and Gwen John or Augustus John, one of our finest portrait painters, as was James Gunn. A portrait of his is worth looking for. John is something of an English legend now, apparently the creator of what Virginia Woolf termed 'the age of Augustus John', his figure linked to such stories: 'Get your hair cut!', a group of urchins called out at him on the street, 'Get your throats cut' was his silencing reply. A source for painting of the Camden Town Group would be Anthony d'Offay off New Bond Street.

The 'Neue Sachlichkeit' exhibition held in 1978 at the Hayward and the 'Paris – Berlin' exhibition held in Paris in 1977 added interest to the German art of the 1920s and 1930s. (Leicester is also an unexpected delight: its museum has one of the best collections of German expressionist art in the country). Bauhaus orientated work has long been popular, Schlemmer, Kandinsky

5. Nu S'essuyant le Pied. Pastel by Pablo Picasso, dated '21.

and Klee: a 1904 Kandinsky gouache 'Abend' fetched £11,000 at Christie's. Works by members of the early expressionist artists or by Feininger are universally popular, but Otto Dix, Heckel, Beckman, Kirchner and Nolde sell best in Germany or the United States, according to Julian Barran of Sotheby's. A Beckman, '*Austernesserinen*', of 1942/3 sold at Christie's on the 27 June 1978 for £38,000. Good sources outside the auction rooms in London are the Piccadilly Gallery in Cork Street, where Godfrey Pilkington

6. Costume design for Nijinska. Pencil and watercolour by Natalia Gontcharova 'Bolero'. Sold at Sotheby's in June 1979 for £260.

often has fine examples, as does Achim Moeller in the gallery in Grosvenor Street. For reference a Klee of 1915 '*Schmaler und breiter Silberrand*' sold for £11,000 at Sotheby's on July 5th, a Nolde watercolour for £8,600, and, going back to the Berlin Impressionists, a Liebermann pastel fetched a modest £3,800. Two drawings by Schmidt–Rottluff sold at Christie's on July 3rd for £1,200 and £1,300. There is still clearly room for the discerning collecter to form a collection in this field too.

Yet another area to be explored is that of wood engravings and prints. Britain has a fine tradition in these areas which Blond Fine Art in Sackville Street has recognised with a exhibition covering the years 1900 – 1960. Edward Burra is a bold individualist in a rough technique, His 1929 *'Railway Gang'* sold at Christies for £5,500 on 3rd March 1978. a Burra *'The Clowns'* woodcut was available at the Blond exhibition for under £200. The range of expression possible with wood cuts and engravings gave artists such as Eric Gill, E.R.W. Nevison or Edward Wadsworth scope for experiments with unusual line, and artists such as Clifford Webb are interesting for the delicacy and detail of English country scenes.

The Contemporary Art market remains the most exciting as it is full of the unexpected, amusing or baffling. Christo, the man associated mainly with projects for wrapping areas or objects in plastic sheeting, is an inventive artist. His *'Packed Edition'* catalogued as 'designed and dated' 63, magazines, plastic and rope' (sic) sold for £4,000 at Christie's on July 3rd. For the ultimate in this art form, and for anyone who finds the lure of the wrapped irrestistable then Sotheby's Parke – Bernet sold a 1963 Claes Oldenburg *'Giant Blue Shirt with Brown Tie'* on the 18th May 1978. Over seven feet high, this object consists of cotton and canvas filled with kapok, with plexiglass buttons and a chromed metal rack with wheels. Although difficult to display, it has a curious charm. It sold for £51,351. His 'Untitled' four pieces of roughly painted plaster suspended from cup–hooks screwed onto a back board, sold for £2,800 at Christie's on July 3rd. David Hockney still remains fashionable and a *'Theatrical Landscape'* of 1965 was sold for £19,500 at Christie's on 28th June 1978, a slight pencil drawing of 1964 sold for £550 at Christie's on July 3rd 1979. The craze for Wunderlich has diminished and Warhol remains saleable, but at the Christie's sale mentioned the two lots offered each sold for approximately half of the estimated prices. The contemporary Art Market seems poised for a development: the euphoria of the 1960's and the early 1970's has evaporated and it is not surprising that with a world-wide economic recession buyers are wary of bidding up on an often relatively unknown commodity, their own taste and thus backing contemporary art to any vast extent. A good example was provided by the sale on 3rd July 1979 at Christie's. *'The Solomon R. Guggenheim Museum (Metalflake)'* a work by Richard Hamilton of 1965/6 in fibreglass acrylic and metalflake, one of six versions of this relief four of which are in museums, was estimated to fetch from £14,000 to £18,000. The securing bid was £8,000. For those interested in collecting only Contemporary Art, there is an exciting variety of talent to be investigated, which can be pleasing even if not of the best talent. Drawings and lithographs of Zsuzsi Robuz show great promise and are finely executed, and a recent show revealed an interesting view of the British Ballet. The drawings of Peter Phillips are also well worth a second look, he has an eye for the juxtaposition of the human form with the mechanical, for collage effects of machinery parts contrasting with the soft shapes of the human animal. Texture is clearly important. The work of Diana Armfield is also typical of the sort of cosy painting much bought because it is technically competent and pedestrian in subject matter, being rather bland. It is the sort of painting which is steps ahead of the Park railing schools, but makes a safe present for an aunt.

All illustrations by courtesy of Sotheby's.

CHAPTER FOURTEEN
In Search of Taste
by Patrick Macnaghten

So various are the tastes of men.

Mark Akenside
1721 – 1770

I HAVE never been able to find anyone to tell me how to define Taste. People are very good at telling me what it is not, and the nastier ones gleefully point out that the fact of asking what Taste is simply shows my own lack of it. That may be so, but if it is at least I am in good company.

'One of the greatest geniuses that ever lived, Shakespeare, undoubtedly wanted taste,' wrote Horace Walpole. I do not know whether he was referrring to the bawdy in *The Merry Wives,* the racism in *The Merchant,* the corpses lying all over the stage at the end of *Hamlet,* or the sewer-like mind of Juliet's Nurse, but I can see exactly what he meant. But was Shakespeare, I wonder, considered to be wanting in taste in his own time? They were robust extroverts, the Elizabethans, and not squeamish in any way at all.

Come to think of it, Horace Walpole sticking all those Gothick turrets on the inoffensive classical building at Strawberry Hill, is not one whose taste can be considered above question.

I was once walking down St James's Street with a friend when a Rolls-Royce glided silently past. It was black, with darkened windows, and the very minimum of chromium plate.

"That car," my friend remarked, "is in such quiet good taste that it's rather vulgar."

If they had had Rolls-Royces in Shakespeare's time I do not think that they would have chosen black ones. A cheerful display of colour to draw attention to their wealth was more in their line. They certainly would have considered it incongruous to put the word 'quiet' before 'good taste'.

I do not suggest that taste is governed by fashion. But I do most strongly suggest that taste is judged by the standards of whatever fashion is current at the time. It is the fashion which changes, and with it the judgment.

But this does not bring me any nearer to defining taste. One could, I suppose, split taste up into categories—Taste in Behaviour, Taste in Art, and many more sub-categories. But in all of them one comes up against the criteria set by fashion. Behaviour, for instance, which would have been considered shocking fifty years ago is regarded as perfectly acceptable today.

I am coming to the conclusion that to define taste is impossible. The standards by which we seek to appraise it are so fluid that they slip from our grasp. It follows, then, that taste cannot be taught. Indeed, this is self-evident otherwise there would be examinations in taste, degrees in taste, doctorates in taste. How proud we should be to write the letters D.T after our names. (It could not be T.D. because that has already been pre-empted by Territorial Decoration.)

But if taste cannot be taught it can, I think, be aquired. But I am not quite sure how. Perhaps by finding out why people whose taste we admire admire the things they do, though I am a little doubtful about that method because of the influence of fashion. A surer way might be to study works of art which are generally regarded as being above changes in fashion, and then analysing what it is we admire about them. We could then apply what we have learned to our judgment of other things. This suggests that learning is important to taste, even though taste itself cannot be taught.

Undoubtedly some have more natural taste than others. But talent is an anagram of latent and it is no good having talent if we are going to leave it lying dormant. There was a time when the most expert cook had to find out how to boil an egg.

It would be nice to think that children brought up in beautiful houses will have a flying start in the matter of taste. But this is certainly not so. Most of them seem either to react against their surroundings or simply not to notice them. Equally, children brought up in ugly houses either react against them, in which case they may develop their taste quite quickly, or simply ignore their surroundings and never develop their taste at all. So taste definitely does not depend on early environment. The matter was summed up by a young man employed at Sotheby's who remarked earnestly, 'You know, Mr Macnaghten, taste has absolutely damn-all to do with class.'

It is all very baffling. In my search for taste I am driven back to where I started. I have known all along that good taste is what we like. Bad taste is what they like.

Quality in an age of change.

CHAPTER FIFTEEN
Glass
by Anne Crane

The glass of fashion

William Shakespeare
1564 – 1616

GLASS a substance that is transparent, lustrous, hard and brittle made by fusing sand with soda or potash or both. This defines the material, the chemical compound, but it gives no idea of its versatility. It can take the form of the drinking glass at your side, the huge plate glass shop front of your local supermarket or the Crystal Palace itself.

In the Antiques world, glass comes in many forms, apart from the obvious glass drinking vessel, it may be a fragment or portion of stained glass, or an 18th century pier glass each of which constitute special interest categories in their own right.

Even limiting the area of antique glass to what first springs to mind, namely, glass vessels for display, for drinking or for eating, we are still left with a vast area to chart. A glimpse at the three most recent world record prices obtained for pieces of glass at auction gives some idea of this range.

In July 1975, Sotheby's Belgravia sold seven items of cameo glass from the Northwood Pargeter collection. Among the seven was a copy of the famous Portland Vase made by John Northwood which, at £30,000 realised a price that was a world record for any glass item sold at auction. Cameo glass manufacture was an art that the Romans had managed to perfect with only rudimentary tools. First a glass vessel was produced. It was then dipped into molten opaque white glass and after the two layers had cooled the overlay was cut away to reveal to a varying depth and tonality the coloured glass layer beneath. The Portland Vase was found in the 17th century in the tomb of a Roman Emperor. Although Josiah Wedgwood produced excellent ceramic copies nobody, despite the wealth of new cutting aids available as a result of the Industrial Revolution, suceeded in reproducing it in glass until John Northwood made his version in 1867. Unfortunately he cracked his own version, or rather the heat of his own hands in contrast to the cold of the outside air one winter's day did, when he was taking it to the British Museum for comparison with the original. Even today, when auction records fall faster than ninepins, the sum paid for the Northwood Portland Vase remains a world record for a piece of Cameo Glass.

In October 1978, however, Christie's sold an engraved presentation goblet dated 1584 for £75,000 and set a new world record. The goblet was made by Giacomo Verzelini, the father of English glass making, in the Broad Street glasshouse and was engraved in diamond point by Anthony de Lysle.

After the 'dark ages' Venice led the world in the manufacture of fine soda glass, This pre-eminence was jealously guarded by the Italians but other countries soon tired of the monopoly and sought ways of unravelling the secret of the manufacture of this delicate substance themselves. In many instances this involved enticing the talented Venetian glass makers away from their home country to work for them. In 1575 Verzelini was granted a licence for 21 years by Elizabeth I to manufacture glass in the Venetian manner in this country and set up his manufactory at Broad Street. The Verzelini glass sold at Christie's is a mature product of the glasshouse. This record was to stand for less than one year however, for in June 1979 Sotheby's when selling the Constable Maxwell Collection of Ancient Glass, obtained a price of over half a million pounds (£520,000) for a Roman glass diatretum or cage cup dating from around 300 A.D.

The cage cup is an incredible work of art, especially when one considers the limited tools of the Roman craftsmen. Even today we are unable to understand the exact method of its construction. In some way, the delicate outer network was cut from the inner layer leaving it freestanding with the exception of a few delicate points of attachment. These three highest prices, then, range from Roman times through the 16th century to the 19th. Afficionados form collections from all three areas and from those in between (although it should be stressed that the majority of important collections tend to concentrate on one particular area rather than ranging over all of them). Those who collect Cameo glass, for example, are not likely to collection Ancient glass as well. Most ancient glass in fact usually appears as part of an auction sale of Antiquities which underlines neatly the point made earlier about the difficulty of 'pigeon holing' a subject as varied as antique glass. In this respect the Constable Maxwell collection was exceptional, largely it must be presumed, because it contained so many important pieces. Apart from the diatretum, for example, there was also a mould blown cup of 1st century A.D. date that was exceptionally rare in that not only was it signed (by a certain Aristeas) but the cup also told us where its maker came from, for the full inscription read '*Aristeas the Cypriot made it.*' Signed pieces of glass are rare enough, but this is the only known piece of

1. A Jacobite glass engraved with a portrait of Bonnie Prince Charlie. Circa 1745.

Plate XIII. A Vienna painted 'Ranftbecher' by Anton Kothgasser.

2. Colour twist stemmed glasses of the mid 18th century.

Romano-Syrian glass to state the origin of its manufacturer. This particular item sold for £75,000 but there was a host of other rare pieces besides, many of which sold for well into four and five figures, so that this particular sale of ancient glass gives one a very distorted picture of that market. The majority of pieces of ancient glass sell at auction for under £100, many for under £50.

The position of later (19th century and more recent) glass is also rather out of the mainstream. Cameo glass as a whole has enjoyed a great upsurge of interest and value and although the Northwood vase was a 'one-off', the prices obtained for pieces of Cameo glass made by the firm of Thomas Webb and Sons from the 1880's through to around 1910–1920, have risen sharply in recent years. One of Webb's finest craftsman was George Woodall who, with his brother Thomas, was apprenticed to Northwood and joined Webb's firm in 1874. Woodall was a master at achieving the infinite gradations of colour and translucency that careful cutting of the glass overlay could produce. In June 1975, in a sale held by Sotheby's Belgravia, a 8¾ins. high plum-coloured vase of c1885 overlain in opaque white with a figure of a girl and entitled *Mischief* sold for £5,800. In July of the next year (1976) at the same salerooms, a three-colour blue vase 10ins. high, c1885, decorated with a figure of a Grecian girl doubled the auctioneers' estimate to sell for £12,000. In September 1979 a third vase, 12ins high of c1885, decorated in white over amethyst with a girl and entitled

Undine, sold in the same rooms for £19,000.

Even the more standard products of the Webb factory have increased in price by phenomenal leaps and bounds. In July 1975, again at Sotheby's in Belgravia, a silver mounted jug decorated in white overlay on translucent yellow and standing 12½ins high doubled its estimate to sell for £950. In June 1979, a similar but smaller (11ins. high) jug decorated with white daisies over chocolate brown doubled its estimate to sell for £1,400. Even a tiny scent bottle by an unknown maker, of 1880s date, decorated with lily of the valley and viola in white on yellow (3ins. high) surpassed its estimate to sell for £210.

These high prices are, however, in part separate from those of the general glass market. They reflect more the renewed interest (which shows no signs of abating) in all aspects of the Victorian era, along with Victorian paintings, ceramics and furniture. In a different way the 'Art Glass' made around the turn of the century and on into the 1920s and even the '30s and '40s has increased at an exceptional rate. The revived popularity of the Art Nouveau and Art Deco styles and a new regard for hand crafted articles is responsible for this and as a result glass by what have now become such household names as Gallé, Tiffany, Daum and Lalique sells for well into four figures.

Two examples will suffice to remind us of this. In February 1979 Christie's sold the Gluck collection of Tiffany glass in New York and a record price of £75,000 was paid for a Spider Web leaded glass mosaic and bronze table lamp.

The record price for a piece of Gallé glass now stands at £104,815 paid for a *marqueterie sur verre coquillage* cup of c1900 at a sale held by Christie's in Geneva in June 1979.

The degree to which this Art Glass is now regarded as a separate category is indicated by the fact that it rarely appears in glass sales but is almost always to be found in the specialised sales of Decorative Arts held by auctioneers with increasing frequency. What is left in the mainstream? What constitutes the bulk of the average sale of glass held by auction? Glass, from all over Europe: Venetian, German, Bohemian, Netherlandish, English and French, enamelled, painted, engraved in diamond point, stipple-engraved and wheel-cut. Mostly it dates from the 17th to the 19th centuries. While dating the pieces is not an insuperable task, an exact definition of the country of origin is often much harder. As mentioned earlier, delicate Venetian glass held sway in Europe for a considerable time but being much admired, it was sooner or later a style and type of glass that was to be copied all over Europe. As such a glass is often catalogued as *façon de Venise* (Venetian style) because, for obvious reasons, it is often impossible to determine whether it is a true Venetian glass or one of that style made in England, Spain or the Netherlands.

Other types of cross-fertilisation also make identification

3. Mary Beilby and her brother William produced this glass circa 1770.

difficult. Fine English lead glass, for example, took to engraving very well and for this reason, plain glasses were often exported, particularly to the Netherlands and then engraved.

As a result one may find catalogue entries describing a particular glass as a *Dutch-engraved Newcastle goblet c1750* meaning that the glass is English and the engraving Dutch. Present-day engravers prefer to use old rummers or goblets because of the softness of lead glass.

With regard to price, however, the general considerations applied to all antiques still hold good—quality, condition and rarity. Each of these or a combination of all three will automatically augment the price. In the case of an object like the Verzelini glass naturally rarity is the factor which overrides all others so that the fact that the foot of the glass was cracked in several places had little effect on the final price paid.

Within this general framework, further truisms that hold good are that fine quality engraving, an unusual shape, special engraved features such as armorials, an inscription or a date (anything that will pin the glass down more precisely) will also affect the price favourably.

In the particular, limiting oneself to English glass, there are some areas within this general framework which have proved particularly popular and which have increased dramatically in recent years.

Among the special-purpose or commemorative glasses one area which proves very desirable is that of Jacobite glass. These glasses were propaganda exercises for the Jacobite cause initially, although they continued to be popular for some years after that ceased to be a real threat to the English. They often bear the motto *Fiat* or *Audentior Ibo* and in addition a number of symbols emblematic of the Old or Young Pretender or both. The most common is the rose with one or two buds, but there may also be an oak leaf or moth. Apart from this they may have further decoration in the form of an air twist or opaque twist stem. These glasses usually date from the 1750's and 1760's. If one looks at a group of Jacobite glasses of this type sold at Sotheby's in a sale in October 1977 one finds that they average out at around £200 each. By March of the next year a similar group offered again at Sotheby's are averaging out at £300 per glass. Prices are even higher for the Jacobite portrait glasses. That is, glasses engraved to the bowls with portraits of the Old and Young Pretender. Two of these were offered in a sale held by Sotheby's in March 1978. A $6\frac{1}{8}$ ins. high glass engraved with a portrait of the Young Pretender dating from c1750 and with a gauze corkscrew to the stem surpassed an estimate of £500–700 to sell for £950. The other glass $7\frac{1}{2}$ins. high and dating from c1745 also bore an engraved portrait of the Young Pretender and a seven petalled rose to the reverse with the motto *Audentior Ibo* and thistle engraving to the foot. This was estimated at £400–600 and was

4. In October 1978 this heavily engraved rummer fetched £750.

finally knocked down for £1,550. The last time before this that the auctioneers had offered a glass bearing a portrait of the Young Pretender was in 1968 when they sold the Smith Collection of Glass and the example offered then sold for £1,100.

These glasses are in a sense interesting novelties and it is from this that their popularity springs. The engraving on them is often of a rather crude and amateurish quality and there are many 19th century versions on the market, as it is easily copied.

The quality of the enamelled decoration produced by the Newcastle artist William Beilby and his sister Mary, is however

5. Three examples of Lalique's *Art Nouveau* styles.

without dispute. This is a second area which is proving very popular at the moment.

The Beilbys worked during the 1760s and 1770s and until about 1970 examples of their work could be found for less than £100. In October 1965, for example, Sotheby's sold a 6ins. high wine glass of round funnel bowl set on a double opaque twist stem and enamelled with a fantastic pheasant-like bird, for what was then a perfectly acceptable sum of £95. In March 1978, the same glass came up for auction again at Sotheby's and on this occasion, realised £1,150, way over the auctioneers' £300–350 estimate.

In December 1975, the auctioneers offered a Beilby enamelled Masonic firing glass decorated with an opaque white floral meander over masonic emblems. Dating from 1770 and standing 3⅛ins. high, it sold for £780. In March 1978 the companion glass sold for £1,000. The increase is less dramatic, it is true, but a Masonic firing glass is a rare thing in itself be it decorated by a Beilby or no. Even more expensive was the Beilby opaque twist goblet sold at Christie's in October 1978. This dated from c1770, its bucket shaped bowl was decorated with fruiting vines and it doubled the auctioneers' estimate to sell for £3,400.

Even the simplest form of Beilby decoration seems to be a sure fire formula for success. A 5ins. high wine glass of c1770, for example, set on a double series opaque twist stem and decorated with a fruiting vine motif just around the rim of the ogee shaped bowl was offered in a sale held by Sotheby's in March 1978 where it sold for £420, well over expectations and the following month at Christie's a similarly decorated glass with a gauze corkscrew within the stem set around with two nine-ply spirals realised £320.

6. Woodall's 'Undine', circa 1880. It cost £85 when new and sold in September 1979 for £1,900.

A third particular area that has witnessed dramatic price increases in recent years is that of colour twist glasses. These are drinking glasses with one of more opaque coloured glass rods incorporated into the more usual opaque white twist in the stem. At a sale held by Sotheby's in March 1978, a group of some eight of these glasses all of mid 18th century date were offered which sold for an average price of around £700 per glass. Apart from the fact that these were excellent prices in themselves, they were also in several instances, well up on the auctioneers' estimates. In particular two lots, a glass cordial (a slightly more desirable shape than a plain wine glass) with two twisted navy threads to the centre of the stem, 6¼ins. high and a 6ins. high canary twist wine glass with an ogee shaped bowl set on a stem with a central core of yellow threads encircled by a pair of opaque white corkscrews, each doubled their estimates to sell for £1,150.

One can compare this last example to a similar canary twist glass sold by the auctioneers in April 1975 for £480.

In September 1979 the auctioneers also had a group of colour twist glasses in their sale which in this instance averaged out at a price of around £1,000 per glass. Among this group was a third canary twist glass of c1760 (6⅜ins. high), consisting of a thick opaque yellow tape, an opaque white gauze and a pair of air threads which sold for £2,100.

These are just three areas in which prices have risen dramatically in recent years. Two warnings should be appended here, however. Firstly glass collecting, like any other form of investment is subject to trends and a trend implies overtones of vogue-ishness. While a certain type of glass may enjoy a brief hour of fame, there is no guarantee that this popularity will endure, a fact that should be borne in mind when one considers items which are currently expensive as potential acquisitions. Secondly, some comparisons have been made here between items sold five or ten years ago and similar pieces sold last year or the year before. In some cases the rise in price seems astronomical. It must be remembered, however, that this apparent leap in value must be offset against the increasing rate at which the value of money is falling in real terms. A piece of glass may seem to have doubled in price over the past three years, but, given the present rate at which the pound's purchasing power is falling, in comparison to ten years ago, the grim fact is that it may only just be keeping pace with inflation.

Colour plate and Figure 5 by courtesy of Phillips. Figures 1, 2 and 4 by courtesy of Sotheby's. Figures 3 and 6 by courtesy of Christie's.

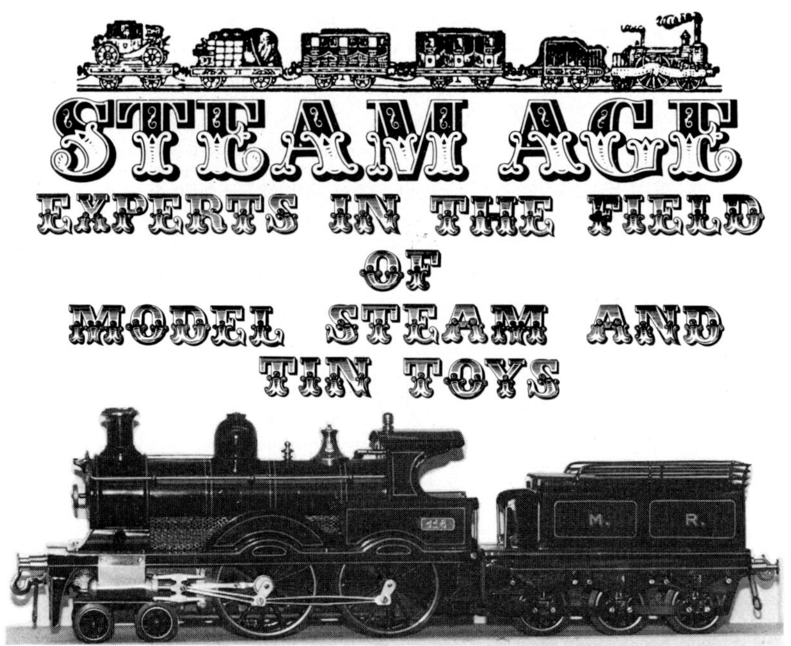

STEAM AGE
EXPERTS IN THE FIELD
OF
MODEL STEAM AND
TIN TOYS
M. R.

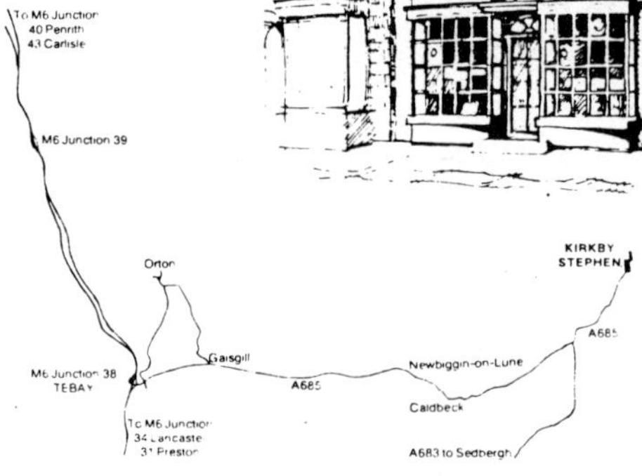

Recapture The Golden Age

with Haig

John Haig & Company is proud to introduce Golden Age, the incomparable de-luxe whisky.

It is a superb Scotch whisky from a treasured recipe exclusive to the House of Haig. It relies for its perfectly balanced taste on a selection of aged malt and grain whiskies; each is a noble character in its own right. The marriage of these fine old whiskies produces a Scotch distinctively different from other de-luxe blends at a price that's expensive to all but the connoisseur.

A new golden age of de-luxe whisky has arrived. Golden Age, from the House of Haig.

1. A lovely example of the unloved. This 1912 Austin is too young for the Brighton run and so not easy to sell.

CHAPTER SIXTEEN
Collectors' Cars
by Michael Frostick

. . . the car rattling o'er the stony street;

Lord Byron
1788 – 1824

THE business of collecting cars as items of value, as opposed to collecting them because you love the smell of hot oil and old leather, is a comparatively recent happening—put it in the early sixties and you won't be far out. An exact date is difficult to find since there is a 'grey period' when the 'hot oil' collectors suddenly began to realise there was money in it. However, like all other antiques and collectable items there is usually some pleasure to be taken other than that of the smile on the face of the Bank Manager; and most people who collect cars, as with people who collect furniture, have some interest in the beasts anyway. It is this interest that has had the greatest effect on changing values, for it is what people want to have, and want to use, that has changed their ideas on desirability—and therefore, of course, on price.

At root it would appear that most men have a nostalgia for the cars of their youth—say just before they were able to have a driving licence. They yearn in maturity for the cars they yearned to drive when young, a fact which may well explain why the richer and more forthright among us collect Railway engines and Fire Appliances. On this basis the beginnings of the car collecting craze are immediately understandable—they were the Veterans—the "Old Crocks" now usually referred to as Brass Age Cars. Before we get too far into describing the different eras we had better look at the official nomenclature—a confusing and slightly dotty subject which only adds charm to the whole business.

Back in the mid-thirties a group of enthusiastic, and slightly pretentious, young men decided that cars were getting awful, and that in fact no decent sports cars had been made since 1930. They therefore decided to form a club to promote the love of the cars they admired, and because they were very young and anything even remotely old could be described as Veteran, they wanted to call their club the Veteran Sports Car Club. That, it turned out, they couldn't do because some older men, with a love of even older cars, had already formed the Veteran Car Club. In the face of necessity they decided to call their club the Vintage Sports Car Club, and laid down that it catered for cars made between 1919 and 1930. If this appears somewhat arbitrary, it was only going along with their elders and betters, who had already decided that Veteran Cars ended in 1904. All this said and done it then dawned on people that there was a gap; and so with scant regard to historical fact, the cars made between 1904 and 1919 were called "Edwardian".

Well and good you might think; but then some of them had "doubts". Were there really no decent cars made in the thirties? They decided, with a suitable show of reluctance, that there must be. After careful scrutiny some of these were admitted to the hallowed circle under the ponderous name of "post-vintage thoroughbreds"—and they were allowed to run up in time to World War II. After that date a discreet veil would have to be drawn. Of course, that state of affairs could not last; there were more young men on the way, and as there were no more titles readily available, they decided to borrow from their American cousins—who had discovered the 'sport car' during the war. They called their cars 'Classics'. This leaves us, in Great Britain at all events, with the following nomenclature:

Up to 1904	Veteran
1905-1916	Edwardian
1919-1930	Vintage
1931-1939	Post-vintage Thoroughbred (PVT)-certain makes and models only.
1945-	Classics. This is doubtful ground as it only applied to certain models. There is no club to arbitrate so it is "by common consent"—or what you can get away with.

One must then beware, for the Americans tend to use the term 'Classic' mostly for cars made between the wars so there is a considerable dichotomy of opinion between the two sides of the Atlantic; and the Americans are still old-fashioned enough to think that 'Vintage' refers to wine and 'Veteran' to people who fought in wars.

For all the complications, however, there is a certain steadfast agreement about how much the things are worth—the higher figures being those favoured by the owners, and the lower by the aspiring purchasers. There is a third price promulgated by a certain section of the trade who seem to have no cash flow problems at all; and having bought an interesting car at quite a high price they add a lunatic margin, and sit, like spiders in their lairs, waiting for the mug to come along. He usually does, pays too much, eventually wants to sell, and is then horrified to discover that despite the ravages of inflation, his prized possession is still not going to make

Plate XIV. Elegance in every Edwardian line, this 1912 Renault fetched £14,500 in January 1979.

even two thirds of the money he paid for it.

From a collector's point of view there are a number of ways to approach the problem, and social habits have had a good deal to do with the ultimate value of any given car. To begin at the beginning it was the Brass age cars—the 'Veterans' that commanded the price. They were odd, they were amusing. A film (Genevieve) was made about the annual Brighton run, and there were other gentle events where the treasure could be shown off. It was kept and polished and rarely used. At this point (and even now) there is a big difference in value between cars up to 1904 (which are eligible for the Brighton run) and cars after that date which are not. Prices of Veterans soared some seven or ten years ago, and then began a steady decline. The best of them can now be readily disposed of for good money, and they have all kept a certain value; but many of them would now be very difficult to sell quickly unless the owner was prepared to accept a 'silly' price.

2. The call of the open car for the open road is always strong. A beautifully restored D Type M.G. of 1932.

The background to this situation seems to be that most collectors these days would rather have a car they can drive about in a more or less ordinary way, something they can even take to the golf club on Sunday morning just to be a bit different. The premium now, is on the years between wars, with yet a later generation coming along who want the best of the immediate post World War II models. A sidelight on this is that the open, or better still openable, car is more highly valued than the saloon. The 'rag top', to borrow an Americanism, is the market leader.

Within these general trends there are, of course, a multitude of different categories. Let's take the money first. There are one or two makes that can be regarded as 'currency'. That is to say they are fairly impervious to the smaller changes in fashion and are always likely to be an appreciating asset. Rolls-Royce, Bentley, Bugatti, certain Alfa Romeos, Hispano Suiza, the big (supercharged) Mercedes, and in America (and to some extent in Europe) Duesenberg, Stutz, certain Packards and probably Pierce Arrow. Here the sky's the limit but you must in most cases go well over twenty thousand pounds for starters—though some of the more ordinary and more hideous Rolls-Royces will go for a good deal less. Elegance (which is a matter to some extent of personal taste) is important here. The car has to look attractive; and a great glasshouse of a limousine on the Rolls-Royce Phantom II chassis (early 'thirties) will not command even half the price of a Barker Continental Sports Saloon, or a Thrupp & Maberly drop-head

3. The best. A 1933 Rolls-Royce Phantom II Continental, coachwork by Thrupp and Maberly.

Coupe. Here the uninitiated must be reminded that before the war firms such as Rolls-Royce, Duesenberg, Hispano Suiza, to name a few, never made a body themselves, and their chassis were always clothed by one of the great custom coachbuilders—and the best of these will always command a few thousand extra on any car.

Outside these *grand marques* are a host of delightful cars which have a more speculative place in the market. Here appearance and rarity will be the true criterion. If you can establish beyond reasonable doubt that the car is one of only two or three made—or indeed the only one—then up goes the price; and if it has stunning good looks that will also help. But there are no rules; you buy at your pleasure and sell at your peril; and there is no living expert who can guarantee anything. The Armstrong Siddeley, for example, excellent as it was, is pretty well without value; but the biggest and best of them—the Siddeley Special—of which only very few remain, is worth what you like to ask for it. But be warned; you could, not unreasonably, pay over twenty thousand for one, only to meet the next day a dealer who would suck a lot of wind through his teeth before offering you 'four and a half'—and you would have to hope he didn't mean hundred! This is the realm for the man who is prepared to buy what he likes—and does not over much mind what happens to its value. In this wild and woolly terrain and there is also some value added on occasion by the previous owner. Royalty usually turn out to be fakes, but Abou Ben Adhem (whose tribe has undoubtedly

4. Battered but unbowed, a Bugatti is a Bugatti still. But this Type 57 is so far gone that the cost of restoration would be astronomical.

increased—in wealth at all events) or, perhaps, the Marschallin Princess von Werdenberg might be a help!

One word of warning in this field—be sure of the facts. 'Believed the only one made—said to have been the property of the Akond of Swat' is the kind of thing that should send you home with an unsullied cheque book as fast as your Mini will take you.

Outside this realm of real glamour and high finance there are many interesting roads to be explored; the 'little black saloons' as the auction boys tend to call them, are not without interest. Here we are always under £5,000 and many of them are neither little nor necessarily black. We're talking of two basic periods, immediately before and immediately after the Second War. The cars of the pre-war period were perhaps rather better made, but rather less fun to drive; though there is something rather splendid about a 1934 Austin Limousine which was original—only the bonnet needed painting. Though some work might have been needed on the engine of such a car it couldn't have been too much for on this particular example it ran very sweetly indeed. Its owner had not been expecting more than a few hundred for it, but if memory serves it ran up to nearly three thousand at Auction—and was worth every penny of it.

There are also odd bargains to be had in this sphere for the adventurous. No one could call the post war A.C. a startling motor car (except perhaps in the matter of appearance where some people thought it startingly ugly) and yet it is full of merit until you try to sell it. They are near enough unsellable; but one day maybe . . . On the other hand, if you have little more discernment, and a strong stomach, you might buy one for peanuts—have much pleasure in running it—give it to your son without incurring any capital transfer tax at all—and die knowing he was one day going to make a packet.

Nice post war cars, the last of the Rileys, for example, are beginning to creep up in price—as are the 'Maigret' Citroens, and it looks as if they will continue to do so—after all they're now some thirty years old. This brings us to the post-war sports cars, which are now a law unto themselves, and a coming thing. Jaguars first. The early drop-head XK 120 and 140 which not so long ago could be had for a song have now moved up towards, if not over, the £10,000 mark. A good Austin Healey is following suit and even the modest little TF MG Midget is now hoping for £7,000 if it is well restored. Few of these cars are original and it is, of course, the cost of restoration as much as anything that has put the price up—so we had better talk of restoration.

We have to thank John Betjeman for

The Church's Restoration
  In eighteen-eighty-three
Has left for contemplation
  Not what there used to be.

. . . and it's much the same with motor cars. There is a certain amount of nonsense here, as the difficult line between restoration and replica is explored. It seems less than logical to claim that if there was one bit of wood left in the old body, it's a restoration; but if that had too woodworm, and had to be thrown away, then it's replica. In fact, the real test is this. If it was once a Rolls-Royce Hearse, and now appears as a boat decked tourer of sporting pretensions, then it's a replica. As long as all concerned tell the truth it has status as a replica; but if someone starts suggesting that it is genuine then the expert (who will be able to tell very quickly) will start calling it a fake. If, on the other hand, it started life as a barrel sided Hooper tourer and still looks like one to-day (preferably with its coachbuilders name plates in position) then it is very hard for anyone to say how much it has, or has not, been restored. If, on the other hand, as a prospective purchaser, you want, naturally enough, to knock a bit off the price it's always a good ploy to say 'pity its been so over-restored'—because this is in any event a matter of taste and opinion, but it does rather spoil the other man's gambit. One thing to beware of here is the use of chromium plate on a car which clearly ought to have nickel—and indeed any other addition or alteration which is not, as the French say, *d'origine*.

One last and most important word on the subject of restoration now that we've reached the 1980s and their attendant inflationary spirals—'don't'. That is to say that the cost of restoring a car

5. Post-Vintage Thoroughbred. In May 1979 this splendid Alvis sold for £3,000.

6. Not a horseless carriage but a reindeerless sleigh. Badly in need of renovation, it nevertheless fetched £460 in December 1978.

now, with labour alone likely to run out at £12 an hour or more, is quite prohibitive and the days when it was worth buying a wreck and making it into something splendid are over. You will spend more on it than you can hope to get back during your lifetime. If you're a D.I.Y. man, well and good, but otherwise the auctioneers' offices are full of eager and enthusiastic men who want an impossible reserve for their cars and are not easily persuaded that the bundle of massive bills in their hand adds up to far more than its market value. Do it for love if you must, but not for business.

So there is it, a world dominated by certain motor clubs whose rules you had best understand before being tempted to make a purchase—for they are the people who run the events which are so often the *raison d'être* of having an old car anyway. But for all that, there is a wide choice and you can become the owner of a perfectly collectable car for anything between £1,000 and £100,000. The choice is wide, the fun enormous; and if you avoid the one or two obvious pitfalls there is no reason why, far from depreciating, your treasured Veteran, Vintage, Classic or what you will, should not appreciate over the years. Within the last year or so there have been no less than three new magazines devoted to old cars—in addition to the two already established, so there is little danger that the fad will fade out and you will be left with a worthless pile of rusting junk. If you know all about it, go your way and good luck go with you. If you don't, or are not sure that you do, then ask advice—it is still a world of enthusiasts and there are plenty of expert minds to help without asking any more of you than that you pay your round in the pub when it comes up. Indeed if there is one thing to commend the collection of old cars (as opposed to old anything else) it is the *camaraderie* that goes with it—and that's practically without price.

Colour plate and Figures 2, 5 and 6 by courtesy of Phillips. Figures 1, 3 and 4 by courtesy of Christie's.

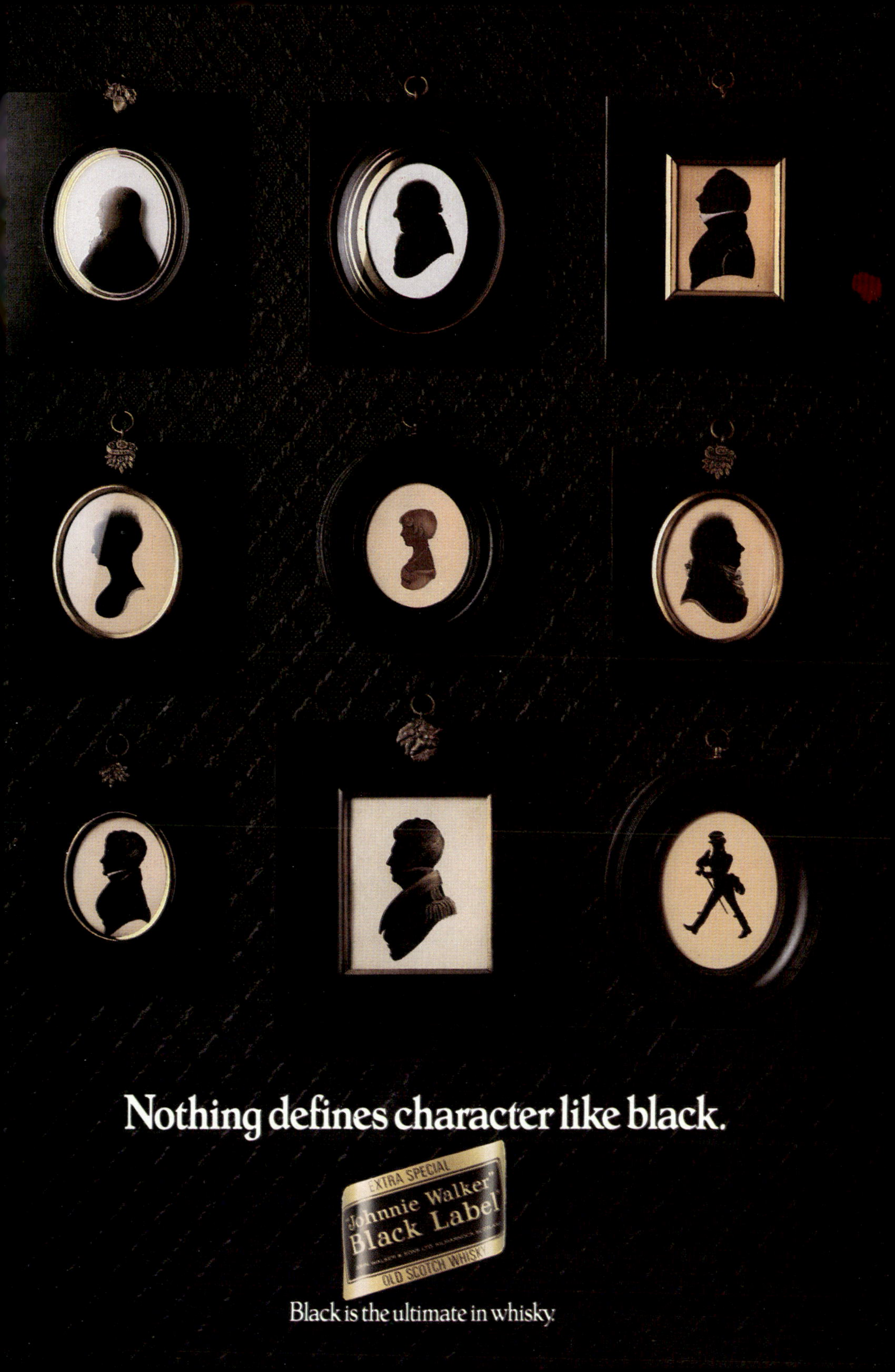

Nothing defines character like black.

Black is the ultimate in whisky.

How silicon chips can help protect precious things

No one can claim complete protection against either natural phenomena like flood and fire or the deliberate damage and loss caused by thieves and vandals.
Alarm systems help minimise those dangers in varying degrees.
Recent technology utilises some classic and well proven methods alongside the most sophisticated silicon chip, wire free and totally unobtrusive equipment.
Wire free systems are more flexible than hard wire methods since the alarm sensor can be moved with the piece it is protecting while its control unit (the part that makes the bells go off or calls the local police automatically) can remain as static as the gas meter.
Arma Systems in conjunction with the American Transcience Company produce a wire free alarm using complex radio coded signals that are Home Office approved in the UK and by PTT's on three continents.
The equipment is currently being used as:-

Personal attack device–a cigarette pack sized unit is carried by the person at risk and when the button on the unit is pressed the central alarm sounds, showing which unit is in distress.

Cash drawer alert–a sensitised cash clip holds banknotes, which when taken out of the clip by unauthorised persons, sets off the central alarm.

Precious Item protection–special sensor devices alert the central alarm that a particular item (painting, sculpture, furniture) is being tampered with.

Shop Alert Button–A system comprising a panic button and a receiver with integral bleeper and reset switch. Ideal for shop keepers and jewellers, to signal a remote warning of a hold-up to another part of the premises.

Fire Alarm–Connected to smoke and fire detection equipment the wire free Arma system can be used to initiate alarms and other protective devices.

Pool Patrol –Floats in the pool and alerts special alarm if someone accidentally falls in.
Especially useful where small children and pets are at risk.

How big is it

Units range from a simple one or two point "shopkeeper" system right up to systems that could cover the National Gallery and still have some spare channels. The costs are similarly diverse, however installation costs and routine maintenance are negligible.

For up to date information on ARMA wire free systems write to Antique Protection Department.

Arma Systems Limited, 26 Cale Street, London S.W.3. Tel. 01-581 1611
In North America: Transcience, 179 Ludlow Street, Stamford, Connecticut 06902, U.S.A. Tel. (203) 327-7810.

1. The 'Star of South Africa', the first diamond to be discovered at Kimberley in 1859.

CHAPTER SEVENTEEN
Jewellery
by Geoffrey Munn

It must be owned, that the Graces do not seem to be natives of Great Britain; and I doubt, the best of us here have more of rough than polished diamond.

Earl of Chesterfield
1694 –1773

OF THE numerous categories of objects offered for sale through the auction room jewellery is one of the most portable, durable and internationally acceptable commodities. It is not, therefore, surprising that in these days of inflation and almost worldwide mistrust of currency that it should prove a very lucrative source of income for the auctioneer. Ironically this trend seems to go hand in hand with an unfortunate recession in the wearing of the more sumptuous examples; undoubtedly a result of a general sense of lessening security for personal property and the resulting prohibitive insurance charges.

The French have two words which separate the term jewellery into two distinct categories. *Joaillerie* refers to those pieces which are set with precious stones and whose value, both commercially and aesthetically, reflects closely the materials used. *Bijouterie* refers to jewels which, despite being made of precious metals and gems, are valued more for design and craftsmanship than intrinsic worth. These words conveniently separate the two aspects of today's auction market.

Recently there has been a notable trend for owners to offer important gem-set jewels through Swiss branches of the London auction houses. Since 1793 when Mme du Barry's jewels were sold by James Christie in London the firm's headquarters have been renowned for jewellery sales. However, in 1968 a branch was opened in Geneva to enable the auctioneers to offer modern jewellery of varied provenance which could not be imported into the United Kingdom without heavy duties being levied on it. Undoubtedly the Swiss reputation for confidential banking of foreign funds has helped to draw the sales of important jewels away from London, its traditional home.

Apprentice jewellers are always told that the value of a precious stone depends on four qualities: cut, clarity, colour and carat

2. Emeralds brought to England by Clive of India.

3. 'Intensity and consistency of colour are of paramount importance'.

weight. Should one of these be significantly wanting then the value of the stone falls, but if all four are at an optimum then the stone is rare and sought after. This has never been more true than in the case of diamonds. In 1974 Christie's had the good fortune to sell a pair of pear shaped stones of 44.93 and 42.50 carats respectively as one lot. In all four attributes mentioned above the stones scored heavily, and achieved a world record auction price for a lot of jewellery 4,800,000 Swiss Francs.

Another spectacular diamond lot in the same sale was the Star of South Africa. It was one of the first large diamonds to be discovered in the peninsula and was instrumental in the opening of the Kimberley diamond mines. A young shepherd boy had found the stone in the dried up bed of a river in 1859 and he was paid 500 sheep, 10 oxen and a horse for it. At a latter date it was cut as a pear shape and now weighs 47.69 carats. It fetched 1,000,000 Swiss Francs.

Diamonds are graded by each nuance of colour which deviates from the finest white, and as a general rule they are less valuable the farther they are in colour from the stone of the purest water, given that the size and purity are constant. However, there are from time to time notable exceptions to this rule. Some diamonds exhibit strong metallic hues and these can exist in nearly all colours of the spectrum, the rarest being shades of red and lilac. There are browns and greens in abundance and sometimes a rich and flaming apricot colour. These gems are widely collected and achieve high and unpredictable prices at auction.

When buying coloured stones other than diamonds, inclusions and impurities can be said to be less detrimental to the value of a lot. This is particularly true of emeralds,a crystal of beryl coloured green with traces of chromium. Intensity and consistency of colour are of paramount importance. An unusually fine and brightly coloured pair of emerald drops, weighing 50 carats mounted with diamonds as ear-rings, was sold in 1976 by Christie's in Geneva for 700,000 Swiss Francs. Clearly an example of the tremendous popularity of this stone in today's market. Emeralds are chiefly found in Colombia but they occur also in Russia and some of the most beautiful were found in India.

A brooch set with highly important emeralds of Indian provenance was offered for sale at Sotheby's in London on 28th April 1978. It was from the collection of the Duke of Northumberland and had been brought to England by Clive of India. (Fig. 2). The larger circular stone is decorated with Moghul carvings of stylised tulips which emphasize its eastern origin and the drop shaped stone is drilled at its apex and may well have been stitched to a garment or used as a turban decoration. The stones were set in open backed diamond frames in the latest taste by Rundell Bridge and Rundell in 1820. Despite their rather unorthodox cutting and drilling the emeralds brought £250,000 from an English buyer.

Sapphires and rubies are precious stones which have almost identical physical and chemical properties. They are both a variety of crystalline corundum, otherwise known as aluminium oxide. All crystals which are not red are considered sapphires, while all red crystals of corundum are termed rubies. Like diamonds, sapphires occur in a surprising range of colours and are often yellow, green or purple. Sometimes gems exhibit two colours in the same stone depending on light conditions, and these, like the famous and rare alexandrite are called dichroic. These are fascinating but are rarely as valuable as their cousins of a more determined hue. The velvety 'cornflower' blue stones found in Kashmir are particularly sensuous gems on account of their unique visual texture and are thus often the most valuable.

Stones of a more delicate tone are very rewarding but less valuable. The remarkable parure of sapphire jewellery which was sold in Switzerland in 1977 for 1,353,000 Swiss Francs is an elegant illustration of this point. (Plate XV).

Plate XV. From a paraure of sapphire jewellery.

Some sapphires and rubies have an internal structure which can loosely be described as crossed fibres. This results in a curious play of light across the surface of the stone which resembles a star. Thus such gems are called either star sapphires or rubies depending on the colour. These interesting stones frequently appear at auction and may be bought for a figure which is often less than the more pure examples of the same mineral.

Whereas a blue sapphire is a corundum crystal coloured with minute quantities of iron, a ruby is a similar crystal which derives its colour from trace deposits of chromium. Rubies, like the emerald, often show more inclusions than their close cousin the sapphire and have a greater tendency to be patchy in colour. A good ruby over 5 carats in weight is considered rare and provided it is of a fine and consistent colour, and is not seriously marred by internal flaws, it is a very valuable stone indeed. The very best examples seem to come from Burma. However, today these ancient mines are well spent and the government has halted the capitalism of travelling gem dealers. Thus a good ruby is probably the rarest of all the precious stones.

A magnificent gem of 26.13 carats was sold from the estate of Mrs Anna Thomson Dodge, widow of the American automobile pioneer in May 1971 for 800,000 Swiss Francs. It must be amongst some of the largest quality stones recorded.

Curiously enough one of the most mysterious, and according to some the most beautiful, of all gems has an organic rather than

4. Later known as the Mancini Pearls, they were given in 1625 to Queen Henrietta Maria by her parents on her marriage to King Charles I.

mineralogical origin. Furthermore it has none of the durable qualities usually associated with precious materials and its age is measured in hundreds of years rather than millions. The pearl has survived all efforts throughout ages to relegate its position below that of its consort the diamond. Pearls were perhaps never more fashionable than at the turn of the last century when ropes like those worn by Queen Mary were valued in millions of pounds. Only in 1921 did the Japanese scientists led by Mikimoto perfect the cultured pearl which was to have such a dramatic effect on the real pearl market.

Possibly the most interesting pair of matched real pearls to have appeared for sale for many years was offered by Christie's in Geneva in October 1979 and dubbed the Mancini pearls. Their weight was in excess of 400 grains and their provenance was exemplary. As early as 1625 they had been recorded as a wedding present to Queen Henrietta Maria by her parents Marie de Medici and Henry IV of France. In her old age Henrietta Maria sold the pearls to Louis XIV who gave them to Maria Mancini, Cardinal Mazarin's niece. She then married Prince Colonna and moved to Italy. From then on the pearls remained within the family until they were sold at auction for 320,000 Swiss Francs. In October 1979, ten years later, they were offered once again by Christie's in New York.

Quite apart from these important gems sold in Switzerland the London salerooms have their fair share of high quality goods, most of which have been in English ownership for some years. This has a twofold advantage to the prospective private buyer. Firstly duty has been paid on importation of the stone or modern jewel by the previous owner and this is not transferable in the auction transaction, and secondly, providing the object selected is purchased at a reasonable figure, retailer's profit is by-passed. This is clearly quite substantial when one considers the amount of money laid out for each valuable item of stock.

However, the prospective private purchaser is rare at an auction since he is faced with the problem of arriving at a price to bid for the lot in question. The auctioneers supply estimated prices in the catalogue but experience quickly tells that hammer prices generally exceed these figures and in some instances quite substantially. Thus the hopeful purchaser is left well behind by the gentlemen of the trade whose generations of knowledge he cannot hope to match. Furthermore he must guard himself against uncatalogued deficiencies, cunning restorations and, in some cases, vendors' deliberate fraud. How can he know that the claw setting of a diamond ring hides a crack to the girdle of the stone which reduces its value substantially? There are a thousand and one similar cunningly placed pitfalls in his path and occasionally the proud owner of a bargain can be proved to be the unwitting owner of a 'pup'. The only course of action is to purchase from a reputable jeweller whose knowledge is quite obviously of the highest. In some cases a specialist dealer in a certain field of object will act on behalf of a customer at an auction, advising on condition, quality and value and will purchase the lot for him. This is a very sound process since the expertise can usually be bought for a fee of 10% or so and the object secured without the higher retail profits. Furthermore the dealer is responsible for his given opinion in perpetuity. When an object is valued more for its place in the history of design than for its intrinsic worth the market can become even more esoteric. Retailers with a certain speciality may not wish to be seen bidding in the rooms for an object since their interest proclaims the authenticity of the lot and may easily provoke competition. Thus a dealer may attend a sale in silence and by implication cast the object into disrepute, whilst his bids are executed by a member of staff in another part of the room. This is a rare device and applies chiefly when more is known about the object offered than is printed in the catalogue.

In the last ten years or so the history of 19th century jewellery has been more widely understood owing to various publications and this has resulted in heady price increases for jewels which had previously been lumped together under the derogatory title 'Victorian'. Furthermore it is certain that some examples which are today highly valuable were only a decade ago consigned to the melting pot for their intrinsic worth. This is another caution for all would-be investors. That which is not valuable today may indeed be sought after tomorrow but exactly the converse may also be true. Pearls have already been cited as an example. The true collector who acquires an object because he finds it beautiful encounters no such pitfalls since his purchase is a joy forever.

In the early '60s gold jewels in the archaeological manner made in Rome, Paris and London were considered commercially disastrous and could be acquired for a price only a little above that achieved for their scrap weight. Today they may bring anything between ten or twenty times the figure needed to purchase them ten years before.

Some of the most beautiful jewellery of the 19th century and indeed earlier is not only embellished with precious stones but also with enamel. This is simply glass fused to metal which owing to the endless varieties of colour available shares much of the appeal of precious stones. There seems hardly a time, apart from our own, when this medium has fallen from popularity. In the early 20th century Alexander Fisher, an Arts and Crafts jeweller of considerable originality described it thus; 'the high quality of enamel, as differentiating it from all other substances employed in the arts, is the great power of its unrivalled colour, and the unlimited variety of its qualities. All the bewildering surfaces, all the depths and lovelinesses that lie darkly in the waters of sea caves . . . these are at hand waiting for expression in enamel'.

5. Cloisonné enamels by Lucien Falize, circa 1880.

Indeed the Art Nouveau jewellers quickly saw it as a medium for reproducing those organic devices which formed such a strong part of their inspiration. On 23rd June, 1979 Sotheby's in Monte Carlo sold a pendant of enamelled gold by the greatest *fin de siècle* jeweller, Réné Lalique. The jewel was a personification of autumn in whose hair are woven maple leaves and fruit enamelled in shades of delicate brown. Interestingly it retained its original case, further decorated with impressed and stained autumn leaves. Such jewels, possibly some of the most technically perfect ever to be made, are very rare and fetch huge sums. They are often included in specialist sales of Art Nouveau.

From 1820 the European applied artists focused their attention on the past and the jewellers of Italy, France and England were no exception. In every way the Renaissance was a valuable source and was freely drawn upon. In the second half of the 19th century there seemed to be scarcely a French jeweller of repute who was not offering Renaissance style pieces for sale, but probably the most famous was F. D. Froment Meurice who was described in his own time as the Cellini of Paris. Christie's in Geneva sold possibly the most famous and certainly the last jewel he ever made. It centres on a carved cornelian portrait of the nymph Arethuse, her hair decorated in the manner of the Italian Renaissance, the chignon set with tiny rose diamonds. The jewel was enamelled by Le Fournier, an aged craftsman who was still very much the master of his medium and one by whom Froment Meurice set great store. It was shown at the Great Exhibition of 1855.

The 19th century passion for the antique encompassed the Greek and Roman styles; that of ancient Egypt, the Gothic and sometimes the Oriental. Lucien Falize, a specialist Parisian jeweller of the 1880s, made the revival of Chinese cloisonné enamels somewhat of a speciality. Recently a set of five gold medallions decorated with flowers and butterflies was sold which amply illustrated his expertise in the medium. Not surprisingly these medallions fetched an impressive £5,000 since they were auctioned at a time when the interest in the history of jewellery design had never been greater.

Certain auction catalogues contain lots of stylish geometric form which were made in the 1920s and 1930s in the Art Deco style. They are characterised by a display of the finest settings and contrast the crisp whiteness of brilliant cut diamonds with opaque and lustrous coloured stones like black onyx, jades and coral. A representative example of exceptional quality made by T. B. Star Inc. was auctioned by Sotheby's in New York for $7,500. Such objects have only recently shed the stigma of being 'second hand' and are now widely collected, occasionally with a somewhat hysterical enthusiasm. The buyer should beware of the title Art Deco when it is applied to thoroughly tedious diamond double clip brooches of the period in an attempt to instill them with a certain glamour in which they are so badly wanting.

One aspect of jewellery which seems even today to be undervalued is the Antique. Those pieces made in Greece, Rome and Egypt before and a little after the life of Christ. This may be because the objects are fragile and not easily wearable. Nonetheless they are attractive and are often technically unsurpassed. Such jewels are not as rare as one might imagine and can be purchased at approachable figures from Antiquities sales at all the major auction houses. However, the warning already expressed to

6. A mid-19th century jewel in Renaissance style. By F. D. Froment Meurice.

prospective purchasers must be intensified in this case. Classical jewellery has been faked assiduously from the time of Benvenuto Cellini to the present day and of this the buyer must beware.

There is a wide range of items offered for sale in the auction rooms which are within reach of the buyer of more modest means. A host of old and second-hand rings and brooches are offered in every sale and the same rules apply in the acquisition of these as for their more flamboyant cousins. Always seek advise unless your knowledge is equal to the trade.

It is not possible to make positive suggestions to would-be investors since this is the province of the clairvoyant. The only advice to be given is stick only to those things which are attractive and well made and draw encouragement from the fact that such objects have always been valued highly.

Colour plate and Figures 2, 3, 4 and 6 by courtesy of Christie's. Figures 1 and 5 by courtesy of Sotheby's.

Plate XVI. Le Pêcheur à la Ligne by Renoir. 'Impressionists . . . works so firmly established that they are regarded as almost above the effects of inflation or economic recession'. £610,000 in July 1979.

CHAPTER EIGHTEEN

Whatever Next?

. . . to conceive extravagant hopes of the future, are the common dispositions of the greatest part of mankind.

Edmund Burke
1728 – 1797

IN PREVIOUS chapters we have sought to show the current trends in fashion for various types of antiques and collectors' items. We now become more ambitious and attempt to forecast the direction which these trends will take in the twelve months following the publication of this book.

While acutely and uncomfortably aware of the folly of trying to predict anything, and with the warning 'never believe anything you hear and only half of what you see' ringing in our ears, we nevertheless feel that by examining the trends of the immediate past we can make worthwhile guesses about what may happen next.

In general we expect the current interest in all—or nearly all—things Victorian not only to continue but to increase. When it was far less pronounced than it is now, some antique shops were optimisticaly labelling as Victorian items made in the early years of this century. But now Edwardiana is established as a period in its own right and the public is paying more and more attention to it. Indeed there are already signs that the process will be repeated, and that interest will soon embrace anything made before the Second World War. That some fine artists and craftsmen were at work in the decade immediately before it has been emphasised by the important exhibition of 'The Thirties' held at the Hayward Gallery on London's South Bank at the end of 1979 and the beginning of 1980, and the founding of the Thirties Society with the dynamic Bevis Hillier at its head.

But there is one trend, noticeable in 1979, which we are convinced will continue, and that is that ever greater attention is being paid to quality. Buyers are becoming more knowledgeable, more sophisticated, and more selective. This is the theme underlying all our predictions.

We do not wish it to be thought that we are recommending 'best buys', from an investment point of view. However, it follows as the night the day that values appreciate as a consequence of demand. Therefore it would be unrealistic of us to ignore the investment factor.

The pendulum of fashion swings the other way too, carrying with it prices and anyone who wishes to buy now with the hope of profit later must judge how far this pendulum still has to go before the swing is reversed.

One type of fashion we confess ourselves entirely unable to predict, and that is the one resulting from a sudden whim. If one of the tyrants who spring up all over the place today should suddenly decide that his prestige depended upon possessing all the left-handed potato peelers in the world the price of such items would rise to meet the demand. But if another tyrant decided that only by outdoing the first one would his own tyranny be secure the price of left-handed potato peelers would escalate phenomenally. Only the death or elimination by revolution of the competitors would stop it. When that happened the grossly inflated values of the left-handed potato peelers would plummet to their real worth. (It must not be thought that we are in any way derogatory of left-handed potato peelers. The editor himself is a left-handed potato peeler.)

At the very end of 1979 two events highlighted the effect of world events on prices. For the first time in history the price of gold exceeded 500 dollars an ounce, and at an auction in Teheran a gold teapot fetched 12 pounds sterling.

Oriental Carpets and Rugs

Ian Bennett has directed attention towards tribal and village rugs. They have only been collected seriously for the past decade or so and we think that interest in them will continue to develop. The price levels of Caucasian carpets in general, certain types of south Persian tribal weavings, particularly those of the Qaṣhqa'i Federation, and Turkoman rugs, may be high now in relation to lesser known types but they may well seem modest in a few years' time.

But perhaps it is in the areas which are not already well known that the enterprising collector should be looking. Not only will he be pioneering a speciality but he will be making worthwhile investments. There are many Middle Eastern tribes who wove rugs, and it is certain that the work of a high proportion of them is not yet fully appreciated, nor has any very serious research been done. Bearing in mind that the concept of intense specialisation in a small area is one of the best ways of reaping long term rewards from the art market, we would advise the new collector who wishes to do something more constructive than merely to

1. Child holding a dog. Drawn by Stefano della Bella, it fetched £2,700 in December 1977.

accumulate a few nice rugs to find a fairly small, homogenous tribal group and then to try to form a definitive collection of their weavings.

Among the more substantial groups he might find worth investigating are the Anatolian Yuruk, the Arabs of Eastern Persia, the various tribes of Afghanistan, the Kurds of North-West Persia and the Kurds of Eastern Persia. The last two, although ethnically identical groups, nevertheless wove very different rugs. The new collector could, of course, specialise in only certain types of rug from any of these groups. We might suggest, for instance, that a collection of Baluch flat-woven artefacts would make a very interesting and valuable collection.

English and Continental Ceramics

Both English and Continental ceramics of the 18th century are highly desirable, highly priced, and in the past few years have shown themselves to be sound investments easily keeping pace with inflation. We see no reason to doubt that this state of affairs will continue.

A more recent development is the increase in popularity of late 19th century ceramics bearing the Meissen mark, though products of the main factory are fetching considerably more than those made under licence elsewhere. This trend, too, we expect to continue because it is part of the general move towards returning German products to their country of origin. Only if something disastrous were to happen to the Deutschemark would this one-way flow diminish.

For any significant changes in fashion we need to examine the areas which are currently neglected, rather than those which are in vogue now. While mid- and late 19th century products of both English and Continental factories are benefitting from the present interest in anything of that period there are exceptions. Those very large vases liberally ornamented with ormulu which were made in France during the Second Empire were making enormous prices four or five years ago. Known to the Trade as 'flashy French', they were highly favoured in Iran. It takes no specialised knowledge of the ceramics trade to see that this market is likely to be less lucrative than it was. There does not seem at present to be any alternative demand and unless there is a sudden craze for such things in some country of the Third World these huge vases are likely to remain gathering dust at the back of the shop for a long time.

But two other neglected areas look more promising. English dessert services of the first quarter of the 19th century have hardly increased in price during the last six or seven years. The reason is probably that they are not early enough to attract the rich collector, and just too valuable for every day use in the average house. However, some of them are very beautiful and make arresting forms of decoration. The tide must turn one day.

Ceramics are fascinating. So fascinating in fact, that one should always bear in mind the warning of Epectetus that a man is a fool who gives his heart to anything which can be broken.

Silver

The forthright advice of John Cooper that 'collectors should be wary of going beyond a rate of £25 per ounce for anything made, say, since 1880 unless it is outstanding' at once highlights the present state of silver-collecting and suggests the turn it may take next. It has become such an expensive hobby that collectors are now severely rationed by price. It is inevitable that many of them will be forced to find new ways of satisfying their instinct for collecting. As for those who buy silver objects for use in their homes they equally will find themselves frustrated by the prospect of a cash outlay equivalent to a capital investment.

We suggest that it is the by-ways of silver which will be explored next, that more and more collectors will turn to categories like napkin rings or car mascots, whether silver or plated. (Already those large glass mascots of the late 1920s made by Lalique and designed to be illuminated from within are collectors' items.) Functional silver will, of economic necessity, be replaced by baser metals and we are strongly of the opinion that before long some of the very good designs, most of them Scandinavian, of the last thirty years will have pride of place on fashionable dinner tables.

Books

It will be seen from Anthony Hobson's very detailed analysis of the present state of fashions in book collecting that the position is by no means static. It would be surprising if there were not considerable changes in the coming months. On the other hand the very fluidity of the present position makes prognostication extremely difficult.

However, we can reasonably confidently express the opinion that anything of German origin or interest will find a ready market. The current boom in incunabula and illuminated manuscripts — especially minor Books of Hours — looks like developing farther yet, particularly because it is international in character.

There are several sections which we feel have peaked and are due to level off, if not actually decline. These include expensive colour-plate books, minor scientific works (with the exception of those by Charles Babbage who invented the calculating machine, and Robert K Goddard, the 'father of modern rocketry'). Thomas Hardy and Bernard Shaw have been very popular with collectors lately — no doubt television has helped to keep them firmly in the public eye. But perhaps they are now due for a decline in favour of lesser known names such as Ronald Firbank.

Finally there are indications that the history of scholarship is a subject which is gaining adherents and may develop into a major collecting field.

Furniture

If we look back over the last eighty or ninety years we can see a pattern in the popularity of antique furniture. It was only in the last years of the 19th century that the Victorian passion for novelty gave place to nostalgia, and people turned their attention to the funny old things made in the 18th century. Not only did they drag the old stuff out of the attics, but they bought new furniture made in designs reminiscent—sometimes very reminiscent indeed,—of a hundred years before. Soon fashion switched to earlier periods, the earlier the better, and by the 1920s Gothic and Tudor oak was in high favour, and the blacker the better. Just before the Second World War, fashion filled in the gap and anything which could possibly be labelled 'Queen Anne' was enthusiastically snapped up. After that war, fashion jumped a century forward and, by skillful promotion by enterprising dealers, Regency was the rage. Being good, elegant, well designed, and well made furniture it has never since then dropped back even though later periods have joined it in popular esteem.

The human race is always looking for something new and with anything Victorian being much sought after, public and dealers alike looked round for a period which had hitherto been neglected. They focussed attention on the only period which was left—the Edwardian. Almost overnight designs which had been brushed aside as being flimsy became delicate, those which had been dismissed as bad copies became derivatives, and those derided as clumsy were praised for their solidity.

Always with the proviso that quality is the most important factor we expect Edwardian furniture to forge ahead. One dealer, typical of many, went so far as to prophesy that a good Edwardian chair worth £250 at the end of 1979 would be worth double that in less than two years.

Like English ceramics of the immediate past, furniture is grossly undervalued when compared with the equivalent product of today. This is a balance which will inevitably be redressed sooner or later and we think it will be sooner.

Clocks

Michael Cox pinpoints a development in clock collecting which will, in all probability, gather momentum. For the present interest in French carriage clocks is based on items which have all the ingredients of a lasting fashion. High quality of craftsmanship, well documented history, and attractive appearance would in themselves guarantee that this is a fashion which has come to stay. But, to underwrite that guarantee, there is the practical aspect that carriage clocks take up very little room. A collector of longcase

2. 'The present interest in French carriage clocks is based on items which have all the ingredients of a lasting fashion'.

clocks can soon find himself running out of places to put them, a dilemma which the collector of carriage clocks will not have to face until much later, if at all.

In fact it is a case of imitation being the sincerest form of flattery that the makers of quartz clocks often adopt the form of the carriage clock, and while this may make collectors shudder their great-grand-children may well be grateful if the collectors lay in a few of these antiques-of-the-future now.

The desire to form a collection is, of course, not confined to the rich. We have recently heard of a collection of some thirty items, none of which has cost more than five pounds and most of them considerably less. They are early wristwatches. Quite a modern invention, the fashion received a boost in the First World War. Uniforms, lacking waistcoats, presented a problem. Unbuttoning the top pocket every time you wanted to look at your watch was a nuisance and officers took readily to strapping a watch to their wrists, a fashion which became almost universal in the 1920s.

Many of the manufacturers of those early wrist watches are still going strong and as yet they have not tired of people asking to consult their records. Though if this new type of collecting catches on as we think it will no doubt the manufacturers will not be so co-operative.

Coins

Collectors work steadily on, never subject to sudden crazes, and few sorts of collectors are as specialised as those whose interest is in coins.

In addition, investors are less tempted to plunge into coins than they are into stamps so that there is no tendency for sudden attempts at cornering a particular issue.

In view of these conditions, we do not forecast any change in the pattern of coin collecting, so vividly described by Robert Darley-Doran. The only change we expect is in values but even than we expect the rises to be uniform, in step with inflation, rather than in one area more than another.

Stamps

Unless the recent dismal performance of shares on the Stock Exchange is dramatically and unexpectedly reversed stamps are going to be more and more attractive to investors. It is, therefore, likely that the true collector will have to pay more if he happens to specialise in an area, such as British stamps of the 19th century, which is popular with investors.

We predict with some confidence that British 19th century stamps will rise more in value over the next year than other issues. Even the rare ones are not so rare that the rich and determined man, whether he be collector or investor, need despair of finding what he wants. All he needs is money and patience. And, of course, professional advice. If he is a collector he will rely on his own professional advice but if he is an investor he would be mad not to seek outside help.

While we think that the stamp market will be dominated by people looking for capital gains we also think that they will miss points which have such fascination for the true philatelist. Their interest will stop short at the stamp and not extend to the cover. Or they may misjudge the value of the cover if they pay any attention to it at all. For instance, an investor when confronted with an envelope addressed in the firm but flowing hand of the first Duke of Wellington might think that he was seeing something of extreme rarity and dip into his pocket accordingly. While such a cover would certainly have a higher value that an ordinary one the real collector would know that the Iron Duke always wrote in his own hand even when Prime Minister, and as the recipients and their descendants tend to keep correspondence from famous figures much of what he wrote has been preserved.

The enthusiastic collector would gain far more than mere pride of possession by acquiring an envelope addressed by a famous personage. He would be encouraged to find out all he could about both writer and recipient and this could lead him down many an intriguing byway of biography.

Nor does he necessarily have to hold in his hand the written word to start him off on his quest. He may be tempted to find out something about the postal services themselves and the personalities who shaped them. It would be fun to list the causes, for example, of the daily routine quarrel between those two larger than life characters Rowland Hill and Anthony Trollope.

Even the most prosaic stamps may lead to a whole volume of social history. One very ordinary stamp was on an envelope containing a very ordinary letter bearing an address in the City of London and a date in 1894. It was simply a short letter from a man to his wife asking her to send the carriage to meet his usual afternoon train on Saturday. Nothing very remarkable in that until one notices that the envelope was addressed to Ruabon in North Wales and that it was posted at 5.15 on Friday afternoon.

From acquiring that one very ordinary stamp could spring a lifelong interest in the Victorian postal system, railways—even the effect of the Ruabon brickworks on architecture.

It is interests of this sort which will keep collectors dedicated to collecting stamps, paying what they can afford when opportunity offers regardless of inflation or investment.

Antique Textiles

As J. D. Mayorcas has shown, needlework of almost all types is being eagerly sought. We expect that, in the main, prices will continue to rise at least as fast as inflation and probably faster. Particular favourites are likely to be the smaller pieces, such as stumpwork and samplers which can be easily displayed in the small rooms of modern flats and houses. As against that, there are still plenty of people with palaces and large houses who are anxious to drape a wall with tapestry.

19th century Aubusson carpets have not 'taken off' in quite the way of other sorts of needlework and as the finer pieces become more and more expensive it is probable that buyers will turn their attention to them.

Paintings I

Old Masters have been in vogue for several centuries and we see every prospect of the demand for superb works of art continuing.

The recent interest in Victorian pictures has rather overshadowed some excellent early works which do not come quite into the 'Old Master' category. Portraits particularly have not kept up with inflation and even artists of the merit of Mary Beale and

3. White birds on the Niger by Madeleine Pearson. Property of the Contemporary Arts Society.

Jonathan Richardson are still relatively inexpensive.

Italian 17th century drawings, often of high quality, are the exception to the general trend of high prices for all drawings. Again, this is an instance of economics dictating fashion for the weakness of the lira means that Italian dealers are unwilling to pay prices which to them seem high in English salerooms.

The most phenomenal change in fashion in recent times has been for Victorian paintings. An extreme example is the artist John Frederick Lewis to whom Jeffery Daniels refers. He was a great artist but some connoisseurs are questioning whether he was great enough to merit the prices his work fetched in 1979 and they wonder what would have happened if he had chosen subjects of less interest to the Arab world.

We think we would be on firmer ground with another Lewis, Charles James. A meticulous draughtsman with a fine sense of colour, his landscapes were fetching between £2,000 and £3,000 in 1979 — a fraction of those of his namesake and we think that they are bound to increase in both value and popularity.

Farther down the scale there are many painters of merit who are almost unknown and whose pictures can be bought for anything between £50 and £300. Two which we think have considerable merit are Keeley Halswelle, particularly his paintings of water (whether in oils or water colours), and H. Woollett who painted farmyard animals on wood around the middle of the 19th century.

4. On the Sands by L. S. Lowry. Dated 1953, in November 1979 it fetched £9,500.

Paintings II

The art market is as bouyant as ever, but as with so much else, quality is beginning to count. The popularity of the Impressionists demonstates this, works so firmly established that they are regarded as almost above the effects of inflation or economic recession.

With Contemporary Art, however, the indications are not so clear. When it comes to making predictions about it our hearts fail us. We have watched with bewilderment the way in which prices have rocketed in the last couple of years. As Michael Pick puts it 'much of the work from the late 1960s not only had a disposable look, but also had a disposable finish which is now beginning to fade or peel'

It is easy enough to see that there will be a reaction even though its timing is uncertain. What is quite impossible to predict with any certainty is what form the reaction may take. It could be towards the representational painting of the 1920s and 1930s, and not only to the great names. Among the chocolate-box daubs of the period there were many artists who never achieved much recognition and yet were painting with charm and merit.

Nearer our own times, the followers of Lowrey into the field of recording industrial starkness are already beginning to lose their appeal, and they may live to regret that they had not studied his landscape work more closely.

There are signs that, as a reaction against the troubled times in which we live, people are looking for gentler works of art and those which require no special knowledge to appreciate them. The flower paintings of the Duke of Richmond are an example of this, quietly charming and competent.

Other charming and competent works may often be found at the Camden Arts Centre in London. The painters who exhibit there belong to no particular school and rather pride themselves on 'doing their own thing'. But they do seem to have in common that they are all efficient draughtsmen. Their excursions into fantasy are based on good drawing techniques rather than, as is so often the case, fantasy being used in an attempt to disguise bad drawing. From such individualists one cannot select any one as being typical because no two are remotely alike. However, a fine example of the high standards to be seen at the Camden Centre is the work of Madeleine Pearson which combines imagination with precision.

Most of her paintings are based on the experience she has gained in her travels far from the tourist routes and verging on exploration. The clarity of her 'personal vision' is interpreted with deftness and skill. We consider that her work and others which display the same qualities will steadily advance to withstand the ups and downs of fashion.

Glass

The enthusiasm for Victorian glass has, as Anne Crane indicates, rather overshadowed the earlier plainer items. While we expect Victorian glass to remain in vogue and to increase significantly in price we think that 18th century glass has been neglected for too long. As the later engraved glass become more and more expensive collectors will, in our opinion, return to the plain Georgian products which rely solely on elegance of shape.

As with jewellery, the individual artists in glass stand out against mass-produced items contemporary with them. Even when their products are not, strictly speaking, 'one-offs' they are rare enough to make little difference to their desirability. The car mascots of Réné Lalique are a case in point. He did not confine himself to making one cockerel but, as with rare stamps, collectors are always on the look-out for duplicates so the price remains high. While many people consider the Tiffany lampshades too mannered for present day taste they are fetching very high prices as collectors' items and we think this trend is bound to continue.

Cars

It would be a very bold investor indeed who selected classic cars as a fruitful area for reliable increase of capital. With, for instance,

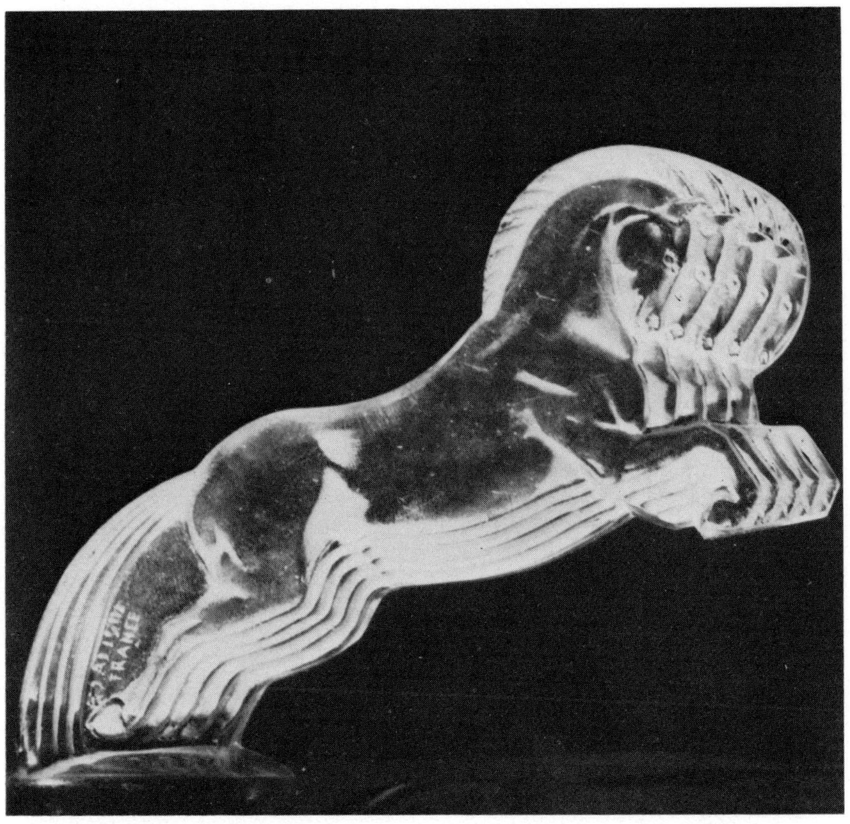

5. A car mascot by René Lalique.

stamps or coins, he can take advice as he would from his stockbroker, make his purchases, and lodge them safely in the bank until the time comes to remove them for sale. But if he tried the same method with a vintage or veteran car he would find himself in trouble. Cars require attention and soon deteriorate if they are left to themselves. Only if the investor possesses a 'heated motor house' can he safely leave his car for long periods and even then it must be carefully prepared for storage. Also, of course, he would need to set the cost of heating the garage against any profit his investment might ultimately show.

Investment in classic cars should, therefore, be left to the enthusiast. He at least can enjoy a dividend of fun even if his capital gain is problematical. The present state of the market indicates that the enthusiast is aware of the investment element (with Silver Ghosts fetching £40,000 how could he not be?) but that he is prepared to let his heart rule his head to a certain extent. This is well illustrated by the attitude towards veteran cars. Pre-1904 cars with and/or on which the owner can experience the masochistic glories of the Brighton Run are steadily rising in price. Cars made a year or two later are hanging fire. They are, says Michael Frostick 'hard to sell—and equally hard to buy because the owners are all hanging on waiting for better days.'

The 'currency cars'—Bugattis, Rolls-Royces, Alfa Romeos, and so forth—are rising in value in line with inflation and we see no reason to suppose that this trend will change. However there are still areas where we expect a kindling of interest and these divide into two main categories which we may distinguish as 'dull oldies' and 'interesting laters'. In 'dull oldies' we include ugly versions of the 'currency cars' and the 'black saloons' of the 1920s and '30s, even if by doing so we arouse the fury of the passionate protagonists of such worthy old plodders as the Austin Heavy Twelve Four.

By 'interesting laters' we mean post World War II sports cars. Jaguar XKs and MG TFs are already fetching up to £7,000 but there are others which have not yet taken off but which we think are due to. Rarity will inevitably be the deciding factor and we think that people will very soon begin to get excited about Jensen Healeys of which few were built, whereas cars like the Reliant Scimitar are likely to be plentiful for several years to come and therefore not yet collectable.

It is rather like politics where yesterday's Angry Young Man sinks into obscurity today only to rise again as an Elder Statesman tomorrow. Secondhand cars decline steadily in desirability—and thus in price—for many years until they emerge as 'interesting laters'. Some, of course, never make it. The mass of run-of-the-mill badge-engineered fleet users' mediocrities die unhonoured and unsung. It is the cars which were considered highly desirable when they were in the first flush of youth which are assured of a serene old age, cosseted by loving hands. Honoured names like Alvis, Armstrong Siddeley can still be bought for something between £800 and £1500 depending on condition and such cars must surely double in value in the next few years.

Cars which are not quite such certain safe bets are the sporting products of the old Rootes Group but of them the Sunbeam Tiger would be an interesting speculation.

As inflation and age gradually—and not so gradually—lift the Hispanos, Isottas and Invictas, indeed all the 'currency cars' beyond the range of the enthusiast's pocket he can be expected to turn his attention to what he considers the second best. Some years ago Austin-Morris or BMC or British Leyland or whoever was at that time fostering the British motor industry's problem child conducted an advertising campaign featuring a beaming young couple proclaiming 'Together we chose a Morris'. Somebody, less reverant, produced a sticker for rear windows modifying the slogan to read 'Together we chose a Rolls-Royce but we bought a Morris.' It is a similar economic limitation which operates in the classic car field. We do not suggest a hearse, or a limousine which looks like one, will ever be either as desirable or as valuable as a drophead coupe or an elegant saloon on a similar chassis. However, we do suggest that the gap between the two will narrow as enthusiasts compete for their second bests.

That supreme enthusiast and connoisseur the late Laurence Pomeroy once remarked, of driving his Prince Henry Vauxhall down a country lane on a summer's day when the hedges were alight with wild roses. " 'This is what God means by the word 'motoring' ". The lure of the open spaces is perennial, and, we confidencly predict that there will always be enthusiasts who will want to take their soul for a drive when the dew is on the grass and the lark is in the sky. Open car, convertible, drophead coupe, ragtop, call it what you will, it is the roofless motor which will steadily increase in value above all others. So, for our prediction of the belle of the ball not perhaps next year but certainly in five years time, we select the Triumph Stag. We are confident that it will to shake its antlers in derision who today call it 'Triumph Snag' or 'Triumph Stagnant.'

From every angle, our advice to the would-be acquirer of a classic-car is this. Go for a pretty one if you can afford it, but let condition be your guide. Except for mechanical freaks like sleeve-valve Daimlers, engines are cheaper to repair than coachwork.

Jewellery

At no time in history has there been as much mass-production as in our own century and it is therefore inevitable that the work of individual artists and craftsmen should stand out. And if, like Carl Fabergé, they would have been considered to be of exceptional merit in any age, their fame—and the value of their products—will reach very high levels. Even so, we think that in a couple of years from now the 1979 prices for the works of this great jeweller to the Czar will look modest.

We see absolutely no signs of a recession in the jewellery market and we expect it to go from strength to strength regardless of the unsettled state of the world. Or perhaps it would be more accurate to say because of the unsettled state of the world. With so many developing countries and so many emergent regimes dramatic shifts in wealth are happening all the time. Not only are the newly affluent splashing money about, they are also keeping a weather eye on the future. There is never much room on a pinnacle, and if you get pushed off it, jewellery is stuff to have about when the time comes to pick up someting and run.

It is not only the insecure—or maybe insecure—who will continue to put their trust—and their money—in jewellery. Wise people who have money to spare are always

6. A Thames Backwater by Charles James Lewis.

looking for something less flimsy than share certificates. Diamonds, we believe, will continue to be an investor's best friend. But we must utter a word of warning. Please go back and read Geoffrey Munn's cautionary tale of the claw of the setting concealing the flaw.

Conclusion

In formulating these predictions we have sought the opinions of countless experts. We have digested and analysed everything they have told us.

But the advice which we have heeded above all other is contained in the words written three hundred and thirty years ago by Oliver Cromwell in his plea to the General Assembly of the Church of Scotland—'I beseech you, in the bowels of Christ, think it possible you may be mistaken'.

Colour plate and Figures 1 and 4 by courtesy of Sotheby's. Figure 2 by courtesy of Michael G. Cox. Figure 3 by courtesy of Madeleine Pearson. Figure 5 by courtesy of Christie's. Figure 6 by courtesy of Phillips.